# Put the F**king Phone Down

## Life. Can't. Wait.

Josh Misner, Ph.D.

ISBN-13: 978-1-0935-5116-7

# UNFILTERED THOUGHTS FROM REAL-LIFE PEOPLE WHO WERE COERCED INTO TEST-DRIVING THIS BOOK BEFORE IT WAS PUBLISHED:

"Hilarious and from the heart, Dr. Misner takes us through the process of an emotional autopsy, looking into our own selves to see what is truly in there, and what we can do to change it in a way that enriches not only our lives but also those around us. I found myself both crying and laughing so hard that I cried as Misner shared his own life experiences, challenging me to confront my own bullshit, and become a better person."

— Christa Skarisky, Stay-at-Home Mom & Aspiring Artist

"This book feels like an actual fucking conversation. It feels like I'm shooting the shit with one of those super interesting people who keeps your attention with one fascinating thing after another. It has an intimate feel you don't typically get from books."

— Jack Parkin, Superdad

"Truly a work of art Dr. Josh Misner has given us in this book. Words alone cannot convey the amount if raw emotion that this book brings out. I am always looking for the opportunity to be and do better. This book not only breaks down the confusion of how to do it, but gives captures the attention of the reader making it a fun experience, even when the experience can be terrifying. Change can be scary — thinking outside the box isn't always easy. Fears of rejection and self-doubt are our own worst enemies, and PTFPD gives you glimpse into Dr. Misner's life in a funny, heartfelt way that connects you. And you see that everyone deals with the same stuff, across the board. Whether you have a doctorate or you are scraping by to make ends meet, anyone can appreciate PTFPD.
Life. Can't. Wait. Read it now!"

— Linda E. Henson, Business Analyst Supreme

"Reading PTFPD will help you to realize what an overwhelming and often toxic force your tiny screen plays within your life. Josh's fresh approach to this increasingly critical topic provides the perfect mixture of hearty laughs and alarming facts in the age of technology and social media addiction."

— Matt Brennan, One Marketing Copywriter to Rule Them All

"In today's age of electronics and our ever-growing yearning for micro-bits of information, this isn't a book you should read—it's one you MUST read. Dr. Misner helps us break the tether that's been keeping us from our children, our families, and the world around us. He does this in a way that is both humorous and enjoyable to absorb. Captivated by his anecdotal writing style, I found myself completely forgetting that he was actually teaching me something, to the point of not being able to…dare I say…put the book down. You deserve it. Your family deserves it, and future generations deserve it."

— Kevin Zelenka, Badass Editor, Families of Multiples

"PTFPD sucked me in on page 2 and opened my eyes to numerous examples of how I am a screen addict. Josh shares entertaining methods of how to replace this mind-numbing screen addiction with effective mindful, all-in experiences. From the very first Chapter Challenge, I knew this was going to be a badass experiment for me, interspersed with plenty of humor and profanity! How can you not take the leap? Josh has woven it all together with personal lessons/adventures with the intent of creating awareness of self in order to reflect on whether you are present in this thing called life — or not. PTFPD was life changing!"

Tiffany K. Aarested, Elementary Educator Extraordinaire

## FOR THE PEOPLE WHO PUT UP WITH MY SHIT EVERY DAY:

This book is dedicated first and foremost to my family.

To Stacie, my partner, bullshit-caller, and greatest inspiration of all time: I fucking love you more.

To my children, those annoying little animals who gave me the motivation to develop, refine, and keep doing all the activities within these pages, I hope I've somehow given you the seeds to plant, grow, and nurture your own fulfilling relationships for the rest of your lives.

If not, blame your mom.

## FOR THE PEOPLE WHO PUT UP WITH MY SHIT THE REST OF THE TIME

I want to gratefully acknowledge all my students — past, present, and future — for working so tirelessly with me over the years, putting up with my neurotic bullshit, and providing gobs of valuable criticism and feedback (even when it hurt), all of which led to the creation of this book.

I also want to acknowledge all the friends and loved ones outside my family who encouraged me, including the early readers who volunteered to step up and help with producing the final product you now hold in your hands.

Lastly, I want to acknowledge you, the reader.
You've taken a huge step in obtaining this book, because it means you actually give a fuck. Keep reading, commit to the activities, and do what you do best.

You fucking got this.

# INTRODUCTION

## IT'S NOT (TOTALLY) YOUR FAULT YOU CAN'T PUT THE FUCKING PHONE DOWN

If you've come this far by opening up this book to the first page, congratulations. In only a few short seconds and flicks of a page (or screen, if you're reading the e-book version), you've made tremendous progress in taking control of your attention span by doing nothing more than putting your fucking phone down in favor of a book. That stated, I'm extraordinarily grateful for the sole fact that you're here reading, because if you cracked open this book, the title for which suggests a well-rounded metric butt-load of F-bombs, then you're most likely the sort of person for whom this book was written.

Let's get a few things out of the way: First, I will freely and openly admit that I am a certified phone addict. I am one of those people who, if I show up to my kids' schools early and have to wait longer than about 37 seconds, I'm likely to reach for my phone. That's probably an exaggeration. It's more like 12 seconds, and I'm checking out. If I'm one or more people away from being rung up in the grocery store (even in the express line), I'll reach for my phone. If I'm at a stoplight longer than 3 seconds, I—oh hell, you get the idea. Therefore, you should know that I'm writing this book partly as a reminder to myself and those like me, but along the way, if I help a few others avoid the same pitfalls as I have, then my work here is not in vain.

Second, after reviewing the shit you can expect to read page, you probably noticed that each collection of chapters begins with the phrase, "Put the fucking phone down and ________." The advice I give throughout this book is all for naught if we can't manage this one simple, yet critically important task. So, let's get used to putting the fucking phone down once in a while, especially when performing the activities outlined in each chapter. I personally recommend having one day a week where we shut down all (or, at least, most) screens, particularly those with which we interact, such as phones, tablets, and computers. I'll tell you the story of how this "technology holiday" came to be later (which I'll tentatively label the "infamous Costco incident"), but for now, trust that we all need to start practicing this simplistic, yet oh-so-difficult task regularly to be successful throughout the rest of this book.

Third, understand that I have great respect for the power of profanity. At first glance, this book may seem like my personal ode to the F-bomb, but I'll promise you now that I wield it and other colorful expletives only when no other words can carry the same impact. I've read too many contemporary books and watched an ungodly number of YouTubers who lack the grammatical chops with which to express their thoughts using meaningful adjectives, and in a desperate attempt to appear edgy, they carpet-bomb their fans with vulgarities. That's not me. I have too much respect for our four-letter friends to dispatch them hastily.

### Who the fuck is this guy, anyway?

You deserve some background if I hope to earn your trust, something I owe to anyone putting in the wrench time to read this book. My reliability as a so-called expert (and I use that term loosely, folks) comes from a blend of two sources.

The first source most people notice is the extremely overpriced three letters frequently found printed after my last name. I earned my doctorate from studying the science of human interaction with a focus on communication and its application to leadership. That sounded way more important than it probably is in real life, but holy balls, was it an expensive piece of paper, so it'd better be worth something. Essentially, I know a whole lot about an exceedingly narrow and specific topic.

Now that you know that, forget it. It's not the more important of my two sources of expertise (again, loosely attributed). What matters more than any book smarts is the fact that each and every gram of material in this book has been marinated in the excruciating pain of personal experience, vetted using raw trial-and-error, and was tested by being either brave or stupid enough to rise up, dust myself off, examine why I failed, and try something new until I finally fucking did something right.

I can spout off all the scientific theory and research in the world, but in the end, which are you more likely to identify with: inflated, self-important, academic bullshit or stories of my struggles from life in the muck? This book is chock-full of these stories, while the lessons from those stories are, in fact, supported by academic research, so I guess we could surmise both are equally important, but I'll leave that to you to decide in the end.

### What now?

Currently, we live in what I like to call the Age of Distraction. This is, without a doubt, the most heavily information-saturated time in the entirety of not only human history, but most likely the world. I mean, if dinosaurs had access to social media and internet, we haven't found evidence of it yet, so I'm going to climb out on a reasonably sturdy imaginary limb that's completely unsupported by any experience in paleontology whatsoever and suggest we're probably the top of the information food chain throughout the history of our relatively little blue orb. To give us an idea of how information-rich our current era is, we need to take a short historical detour to look at how we arrived at this point.

Buckle up because this is where shit gets real.

## Viva la Revolution!

As of this writing, most communication scientists agree that humanity has suffered its way through four major revolutions in the way we interact with one another, and each of these was triggered by a big-ass innovation to the tools with which we humans communicate. In fact, the fourth revolution is the one in which we're currently embroiled, but we'll cross that bridge later.

### *Revolution #1: The Alphabet*

The first of these four revolutions came about because of writing, and before anyone calls bullshit on me, think about it for a second. Homo sapiens graduated from being purely oral cultures (people who only use talking to communicate) to becoming societies with writing at various points along their respective timelines, and depending on which culture we're looking at, this may have happened anywhere along a spectrum lasting several millennia. Cultures throughout the world were not yet connected by the internet (see my earlier note regarding dinosaurs), so this form of communication technology had to develop both organically and independently within each of those cultures. It isn't like they were subscribing to one another's newsletters, especially since they didn't yet have a written alphabet.

Think about this for a second. What was life like for a purely oral culture? There were no books, so everything we're reading now would have been information passed along by some person talking out the whole goddamn thing. In fact, professional storytelling was a career path back then. Think about it – some dude or dudette wandered from one town to the next, getting paid to stand around the campfire and retell the story of the fall of Troy.

Look, I used to get in trouble every damn day for talking too much while working a fast food job, but I can't even remember my goddamn grocery lists most of the time (a story of which I'll save for later), so I can't even begin to fathom the mad memorization skill it must have taken to pull that off. Of course, without Netflix and Hulu, entertainment options were somewhat limited, so it seems like these folks were pretty popular when they showed up in town.

Still, the advent of writing changed the fucking world. It was responsible for vaulting the importance of contracts over handshakes and verbal agreements. It was responsible for recording and storing of records, which later helped keep politicians more accountable, and it helped storytellers preserve some of the most important tales for future generations. Ever read *The Iliad*? That shit was passed down orally for generations before ever being printed. Writing allowed humans to start sending private messages over long distances, and it helped assclowns like me remember what they needed to pick up from the store on the way home from work.

Not everyone was thrilled about writing though. A particularly cranky Greek dude by the name of Socrates (bonus points if you read that in character, a la Ted from *Bill & Ted's Excellent Adventure*), predicted it would be the downfall of humanity. Too many people, he suggested, would start relying solely on the written word, and next thing we know, there would be a whole generation of forgetful idiots. Honestly, I feel attacked by that statement, but I think we, as a society, are doing pretty damn well for ourselves despite shitty memories like mine. Think his argument sounds familiar? With every revolution in communication, there are naysayers who think that the changes we face will be the downfall of humanity, even though we've been pretty fucking awesome at adapting so far.

Remember this: As we progress through the rest of this historical field trip, you will notice that there are winners, and there are losers. Each time society changes, some people benefit more than others, and it's almost *always* the ones who refuse to adapt until it is too late that end up becoming history's losers.

### *Revolution #2: Mass Production*

A few thousand years after the first revolution with the written word, a second revolution started with the printing press or, in more general terms, the mass production of written communication. Shortly before the first millennium BCE was up, the Chinese invented wood block printing to mass-produce artwork, and after that, Koreans invented metal moveable type in the late 14th century. However, these printing presses failed to revolutionize the Asian world in the same way that Gutenberg's invention of moveable type would later revolutionize Europe. This probably had more to do with the complexity of Asian typography than the invention in general though. The concept of inventing a device to mass-produce written information seems so obvious and simple to us today (seriously, my 11-year-old thought of it when he was like 7, at which point I had to inform him that he was about a half-millennium too late), but at the time, the concept was so revolutionary that it radically transformed the European world, almost overnight.

Johannes Gutenberg's invention in the mid-15th century reduced the cost of production, which increased the availability of information. Higher availability led to increased literacy rates, and as that happened, the common folk of the time suddenly realized how they had been duped and manipulated all along by the church, the wealthy, and anyone else who could read and afford books. Remember, those who control the flow of information are those who possess *real* power.

Much more than an information revolution broke out, and next thing everyone knew, the Christian church split down the middle into Protestants and Catholics, and fighting between the two continues today in certain parts of the world. In addition to all-out revolution, humanity also enjoyed the many benefits of the Enlightenment, out of which was born many of our modern philosophies, sciences, and ways of thinking. Hell, most modern educational systems are still being modeled after those found in the Enlightenment. It's hard to believe little metal blocks could lead to such a drastic change, but they did.

Now, this part is important: I want us to remember the distance in time between the first revolution—*the written word*—and the second revolution—*mass production*—was around 4000 years, depending on which cultural story we're looking at. It took humanity all of four thousand years to come up with an idea as simple as moving metal blocks and ink to quickly reproduce information, but the next revolution would cut that distance in time by a factor of 10.

### *Revolution #3: Industrial Revolution*

Only 400 years after the second revolution in communication came the dawn of one of the most drastic series of inventions to change humanity in all its sordid history. Beginning in the early 1800s, one invention after another littered the landscape of industrialized society, each separated by a mere handful of years. So, why did the distance between revolutions reduce by a full order of magnitude? The answer is relatively simple: With more information available, smart people took advantage of this knowledge and used it to spawn even more brilliant ideas, which then multiplied even further as they spread. You know that feeling we often get with respect to the rate of new technology speeding up, and we feel like we can't even keep up with all the new advances? This was where it started. Blame our recent ancestors and their overactive brains.

I often like to think of what centenarians have witnessed over their lifespans. As of this writing, in late 2018, the oldest verified person in the world was 122 years old. Her name was Jeanne Calment, and she was born in France in 1875. She was 28 when the first human took flight on a windy beach in North Carolina, and by the time she turned 53, the first black-and-white television hit the market! She was 61 when the first computer started solving simple math problems, 72 when the world changed radically as the first transistor allowed humanity to shrink electronics from something that took up an entire fucking warehouse to a gadget that fits in the palm of one's hand, and when she celebrated her 82nd birthday, the first satellite was launched into orbit. By the year of her 109th birthday, she could have bought her first home computer and cell phone with a large enough fortune, but the real kicker was when she turned 116, and the world was revolutionized by the miracle we now know call the world-wide web.

After considering all that, please forgive me for a gratuitous, yet well-earned — holy fucking shit! That's a mind-blowing life story if I've ever heard one, and we only examined the timeline in which she lived. We didn't even get around to exploring her personal life history, which I'm sure is one of the most interesting tales one could explore.

Such was the impact of the Industrial Revolution, or at least as far as its influence on communication. Humanity never really had a chance to catch its collective breath and grow accustomed to life with all these new conveniences. Hell, by the time we finally figured out television's effects on individuals and families, the internet started fucking with our heads, and now we have no idea what in the psychedelic hell is happening to us. Our ancestors had four goddamn millennia to adjust to writing and four freaking centuries to get used to the impact of the printing press, but our generations?

Let's do the math: 4000 divided by 400 gives us 10, so divide that by 10 again, and we get 40, right? Not even fucking close. Information has been flying around profusely, and thanks to the strength of modern educational systems (okay, sure, they have their faults, but look at the end product here), we entered the fourth revolution somewhere around the early 2000s. If we peg the end of the third revolution somewhere around the advent of modern transistor-powered electronics, we should have gotten about a 40-year break, but I've been alive through nearly that whole period, and I haven't felt a single fucking break yet. How about you?

### *Revolution #4: What the Holy Hell is Happening?*

Some theorists suggest the most current revolution started with computers, but my first experience with computers was using them to type out naughty words in the word processing software in the computer lab at my high school and giggle relentlessly or learn how it feels to consistently and repeatedly bang my head on the keyboard after dying of dysentery during Oregon Trail (fording those fucking oxen over the river got me every time). Personally, I think computers are merely another tool; their existence and proliferation wasn't the sole source of a revolution.

Other theorists propose that the revolution started with the advent of the interwebz. In 1991, a British dude by the name of Tim Berners-Lee effectively invented the "world-wide web" as we know it today, and it exploded in popularity and usage. But, despite all the flashy Geocities sites (even the ones that automatically loaded a rockin' glam metal MIDI and JavaScript glitter bombs that followed your mouse around the screen), the buzz of a 56.6K modem dialing up, and a whole stack of free AOL trial CDs didn't change the world. But, it was getting closer. If you're reading this, and you're under the age of 25, I'm guessing none of that made sense.

Most social scientists, myself included, now theorize that it was the *convergence* of all our emergent technologies that brought about the most radical shift in life atop the blue marble. Computers + internet + mobile connection + social networks = a level of even with which most of us can't. Pause there for a moment, because I have a separate but poignant point to make before we continue.

If fish were cognitive and salient beings that could talk to us, that would be weird. I mean, if my goldfish suddenly struck up a conversation with me, I'd be extensively creeped out, especially since I don't have a goldfish, but for the sake of the analogy, let's pretend I do have one, and it can talk. If you could talk to my pretend fish and not feel like you were utterly bat-shit crazy, then how would you explain water to that fish?

Whoa.

Mind blown, right?

Maybe you've heard that saying before, as it was mentioned in a famous commencement speech by David Foster Wallace, but let's think about it in terms useful to our argument. The collective whole of humanity is seated smack-dab in the middle of ground zero with respect to the biggest fucking communication revolution to ever hit our planet, which has had the same impact on society's communication as a nuclear warhead would have on, well, pretty much anything made up of atoms. We are surrounded by so much rapid change that, for us to adequately explain what in the actual fuck is happening, as it happens, is pretty difficult, even for those of us with those three little fancy letters after our names.

Okay, un-pause and let's address the question of, "what in the actual fuck is happening to us?" Simply put, we don't know where we are or what we're doing, and we sure as shit don't know where we're going to end up, even within the next five years. Lots of theories try to explain and make sense of it all, but most of them end up disproven or need extensive edits as time unfolds, so even the smartest of us are trying to figure things out as we go, and that's a pretty scary thought if we ponder it much longer than a few minutes.

That's why a book like this is so important. Even if I don't know exactly what's happening and none of us can effectively and accurately predict where we're heading, what I can offer us in the way of a lesson is how to manage the way we react to these changes right here and now. Mindful, intentional control over our behaviors will most likely be our greatest saving grace as we navigate the waters of these turbulent and uncertain seas. A common analogy to the act of trying to find and use information in our time is like trying to get a drink from a fire hose. We are no longer merely passive information consumers; we have shifted more toward a consumer/producer model, where anyone with access to technology and a network connection can produce and share new information. With all that information flying around, constantly shouting, "LOOK AT ME! LOOK AT ME!" we find ourselves under a constant state of duress and our attention spans yanked in every direction at once, which makes it difficult to focus on that which really matters.

To test this out, I'm going to ask for your participation in the first of several "Chapter Challenges," and this one requires a pen or pencil, so go grab one.

Don't have one?

No worries.

Go get one.

I'll wait here.

Got one now?

Okay, good.

What I want you to do is this: As you read the next section of this chapter, I want you to make a little hash mark in the margins every time a thought pops into your head other than what you're reading. And I mean EVERY last insignificant thought that shows up in your consciousness if it isn't what you read from the text. Even if you end up thinking about how difficult it is to not think about anything else, then that thought still pulled you away from what you are reading, so make a hash mark. If, while making a hash mark in the margin, you suddenly think, "this exercise is really fucking stupid," then make two hash marks: one for the random thought that popped up and another one for calling my awesome activity stupid.

It's a lot like when someone tells you not to think of a pink elephant. Close your eyes, and what do you immediately see? That's right, a pastel pachyderm. Play along and be honest with yourself. Also, don't be a chicken-shit bibliophile who says something like, "I respect books too much to write in them." Be rebellious. Make the hash marks. There's a point to all this, and it will definitely become clear later in the book why I'm asking you to violate these pages.

Let's do this…

### *The Information Age*

As I was researching academic journal articles in a feeble attempt to put our modern problems into perspective (there's at least one hash mark – nobody reads a sentence like that without thinking about how dull it's about to become), I ran across a shiny, brand-new, super-expensive word: zettabyte. If you aren't familiar with geek-ese, a byte is eight bits, and a bit is a 1 or a 0, which forms the foundation for all modern computing. Most contemporary computers as of this writing have a storage space of around one terabyte (ish), which is about one trillion bytes (roughly 8 trillion ones and zeroes). Hell, my iPhone X has 256 billion bytes of storage, and yes, I did spring for the X shortly after it broke the $1K phone barrier, so make three hash marks for being so judgmental about my life choices. An average picture on my phone is about one megabyte, or about one million bytes.

However, a zettabyte is this many:

1,000,000,000,000,000,000,000

Yes, that is a 1, followed by 21 motherfucking zeroes. To put this in perspective, that's one billion terabytes or if you prefer to count like my kids do, then it's a thousand-billion-billion bytes. If we had a couple of shit-tons of 1TB SATA hard drives (the hard drive likely doing the work inside your computer) and placed them flat on the ground, end-to-end lengthwise in a single-file line, we'd have a line that stretched around the equator of our planet almost eight times before we had a total of one zettabyte worth of storage. Of course, we'd lose a majority of them because they don't function well after being immersed in the ocean, but for the purpose of this thought experiment, let's pretend we have a magical land bridge all the way around the middle of the planet. The retail cost of all those hard drives would be around $45 billion, plus tax, based on 2018 Amazon prices.

What does this all mean? If you're like me, then maybe it feels too big to comprehend, so let's get some perspective.

The entirety of all human speech ever spoken throughout the history of our species through the year 2003, if it was transcribed into a text file, would be roughly equivalent to 5 exabytes. That's 5 million TB, which sounds like a lot, but only 0.005 zettabytes.

According to a report published by The Guardian, by the time the web turned 18 in 2009 and could legally vote (but still chose not to, much like the shameful half of the eligible voting U.S. population in recent years), the entirety of the internet at the time contained half a zettabyte, or 500 exabytes.

A mere two years later, in 2011, according to the International Data Corporation, that number multiplied by six to a total of 3 zettabytes.

Conservative estimates are that, by 2025, humanity will have created and digitally stored nearly 200 zettabytes.

That's what I call a seriously big fucking fire hose from which to attempt to quench our natural human desire for knowledge, and it's not letting up anytime soon.

There is no question that, upon looking at these statistics, our species dove headfirst into the Information Age. We are now creating and sharing information at a rate too high to adequately consume, and this generates an unintended byproduct. Humans are now experiencing a high degree of latent anxiety with respect to which information we should consume. It's like being really fucking hungry, heading to a buffet for dinner, but then discovering that literally every possible food choice is present.

It's growing increasingly common for people to feel overwhelmed by the enormity of all this data and never-ending flow of information, but I also imagine this may have been how it felt to live during one of the previous three revolutions. It's pretty damn scary to see the world we know upended and everything we know changing in front of us, but we need to remember that, as I mentioned before, there are winners and there are losers emerging from each revolution.

The winners are those who embrace the revolution for what it provides, adapting to the changes as needed, such as philosophers who jotted down their ideas instead of shunning writing, entrepreneurs who saw an opportunity to educate common, everyday people after the printing press, and even the lucky asshole who had the foresight to purchase the domain name "insurance.com" when the internet exploded and then sold it for $35.6 million in 2010.

The losers, on the other hand, are those who remain firmly rooted in outmoded ways of thinking, such as oral storytellers, calligraphers, and the people who held out and refused to buy a touchtone phone until manufacturers finally put their collective corporate feet down and said no more.

Simply put, the strong adapt to survive, and thus, so shall we. Richard Saul Wurman famously stated back in 1989 that, "A weekday edition of The New York Times contains more information than the average person was likely to come across in a lifetime in seventeenth-century England." He also suggested that, to be a successful member of modern society, we must "assimilate a body of knowledge that is expanding by the minute."

Still marking up the margins with those hash marks? Maybe you started drawing pink elephants by now. Either way, don't forget to chalk up each and every last thought other than what you're reading here, and be honest!

Humans have a notoriously inherent biological need to both be social and to consume information. Today, we feed this craving with our mobile devices, plugging ourselves into a global network along with billions of other humans and using this network to Google everything from how black holes are formed to why cats purr. This affords us the opportunity to not only consume and create new information, but also to share it, thereby adding another layer to our role in this revolution by allowing us to reproduce information as well. Propagation of information is now what we do best and most often, even if that information is as seemingly useless as a meme of a cat wearing a birthday party hat and pretending to play Africa by Toto.

We all know by now that the internet was created for the sole purpose of sharing cat memes. Everything else is mere noise.

As a result of the ease of creating and sharing information, we have at our fingertips a 24/7 flow of endless information, not all of which holds value, I might add. According to 2019 YouTube statistics, 300 hours of video are uploaded every minute of each day, which adds up to about 2.6 million hours of video each year. Obviously, there's no way for one person to watch all that (though I swear my kids try), so where do we place our attention? If you answered that question in your head, jot down another hash mark.

Attention is the hard part. As much as we'd like to delude ourselves into believing we have total control over our attention spans, we don't. Thanks to sophisticated, complex, and downright devious marketing techniques, our attention spans end up drawn and quartered in the resultant brawl. According to the American Marketing Association, the average consumer is assaulted with about 10,000 brand messages every day (not that we could possibly comprehend that many), and a British study found that the average person switches between screens about 21 times an hour. This endless shit-storm of information pummeling away at our attention spans during each waking moment (and yes, even sometimes while we sleep) has elevated time and attention to more valuable commodities than our dollars could ever provide. Life amid the Age of Distraction may have made some aspects easier, but with respect to finding information, it has not made getting a drink from the proverbial fire hose easier; it has only provided us with more hoses from which to choose, all while cranking up the water pressure of each one to a deadly level.

As a result, we now live in what's called an *attention economy*, which was predicted way back in 1971 by the economist, Herbert Simon. He proposed that a wealth of information would produce a scarcity of attention. Simply put, information consumes our attention while it is digested. With more consumption of information, we become impoverished with respect to attention, and as such, we need to become pickier with where we direct that attention.

With greater stress being placed on our attention spans, they end up stretched thin and increasingly fragile, and as entities compete ruthlessly for our attention, the likelihood of losing control over these spans increases drastically. This process occurs slowly enough to where we become like the disturbingly twisted old analogy of the frog in the pot of boiling water, and before we know what happened, stress and anxiety levels have spiked out of control, leaving us bewildered as to the cause. Distractions permeate even our most intimate moments, thereby reducing opportunities to shut down, tune out, and recharge.

### *The Age of Distraction*

The Information Age has us drowning amid vast seas of information, but with all this power also comes potential for disaster. Way back in the 1930s, famous social scientist, psychology researcher, and renowned torture-master of rodents, B. F. Skinner, conducted experiments on rats to determine how behaviors are formed. In his now-infamous "Skinner Box" experiments studying operant conditioning, Skinner found that, when he put a rat in a box with a lever that spit out a food pellet as a reward every time the lever was pressed, the rat would eat while maintaining reasonable restraint. It wasn't until Skinner randomized the reward and removed the rat's ability to predict when food came out that the rodents became incessantly obsessed with pressing the lever. Because the rats weren't sure when their next meal was going to come out, they pushed the lever uncontrollably like furry little crackheads and ended up overeating without realizing how their behavior changed. Essentially, this sick bastard would later become the inspiration for Candy Crush without even knowing it.

Operant conditioning probably sounds familiar because we're all being conditioned like this on a daily basis. Sure, that may sound a bit like justification for tinfoil headgear, but the next time your phone vibrates, pay attention to what you do. Do you immediately reach for it, salivating like Pavlov's dog at the dinner bell? How about when you're writing a paper, reading this book, or responding to an email, and the ever-familiar chime of a social media notification rings out?

These bells and whistles are our modern equivalent of Skinner's lever. We drop what we're doing, refocus our brains, and divert our attention elsewhere, which is basically no different than our distant mammalian cousins infatuating over a fucking lever. The more these levers exist within our normal routines, the greater the potential for distraction we have to live with, and the more work we'll need to do to regain control. If seeking information in the Age of Distraction is like getting a drink from a fire hose, then trying to resist those temptations feels like salmon swimming against Class V rapids.

But, this is precisely our task, and swim we shall, despite the hopeless enormity of it all. Things like zettabytes and knowing that we're exposed to more than 10,000 brand messages a day? Those numbers exist no matter what we do or don't do, so it's best to simply accept that they are out there.

Once we do that, we can stop fighting against the current and float gracefully without a single fucking care in the world.

If this sounds good, put the pen or pencil down and stop with all the hash marks.

Go back through the chapter and take it all in. No need to count them all; a quick scan is fine. Are you surprised? Do you remember making all those marks? Better still, do you remember what you read, or do you need to go back through and read it all over again to actually comprehend what you read? Frustrating, isn't it? What do these hash marks tell us about how much our minds control us, rather than the other way around?

This is what we go through each and every day, only we are most likely unaware of this process. If it's true that we switch screens 21 times an hour, then that's a total of 336 glances at our screens throughout the day, presuming a 16-hour day. What if I glanced at my wife 336 times instead? Okay, that's creepy, so maybe I should divvy it up. Two of my kids still live at home, and the other two I can text or call. If I divide it evenly, what if I were to reach out to each member of my immediate family 67 times a day, or about 4 times each hour per person? They'd be pretty fucking annoyed and might want to tell me to shut the fuck up, but you get the idea. What if even part of the time and attention we wasted on our screens was instead devoted to those we love or to more worthwhile activities we've always said we simply don't have the time for?

## What Next?

The ultimate goal of this book is to regain control over our attention spans so that we can make mindful, deliberate, and intentional decisions on where that attention goes. To achieve that goal, this book is based on the foundational keys to emotional well-being published by the Center for Healthy Minds in the University of Wisconsin-Madison: *Awareness, Resilience, Savoring, and Connecting.* See? I told you I had some actual research to back up all my bullshit.

Within each of the major sections of this book are individual chapters, and in these, there will be at least one Chapter Challenge to complete. Trust me when I state confidently that you will get far more satisfaction, development, and serious personal growth out of this book if you complete each and every one of them as directed. Of course, I can't be there to enforce the activities, and if I was, that would also be pretty fucking creepy, so we're going to be working off the honor system here.

Understand that not every Chapter Challenge will be profound and life-changing.

Many will be difficult.

Others will wrap you with you a serious case of the warm rainbow-kitten-puppy-unicorn fuzzies.

Depending on your background and personality, some might even be "meh, that was a thing."

But, each one fits within one another like pieces in a puzzle, and unlike a typical puzzle, you have no picture on the box to see what the final product looks like, so by completing each one, you will slowly start to see how it all comes together.

Approach each Challenge with courage, curiosity, and conviction, and when we arrive at the final page together, I guaran-fucking-tee you will have experienced something powerful. If that sounds like a lofty goal, I suppose it is, so let's get to work.

# PART I:

## PUT THE FUCKING PHONE DOWN & LOOK AROUND

In this first section of the book (Chapters 1-3), we're going to explore what it takes to become more self-aware. After all, what the hell good is the pursuit of a better life without knowing where to begin? We'll explore tools and activities that nurture more consistently mindful habits, and some of these are understandably uncomfortable. Putting the fucking phone down is a bit like putting down a crack pipe, heroin needle, or vaping thingy I see so many kids using today. It's certainly not my intent to make light of difficult substance addictions, but the psychological addictions created by the abuse of electronics produces so many of the same withdrawal symptoms we see showing up in other addictions. Changing this lifestyle isn't easy, so we need to develop the skills to cope with those changes, or we run the risk of none of our efforts sticking.

In addition to exploring how to become more mindful, we'll also examine various listening styles and learn more about how those styles can be changed consciously and deliberately, depending on the needs of the situation. Listening comprises half of the communication process, and honestly, it's probably the more important half by a long shot. Not knowing how to listen effectively is a potentially ginormous fucking barrier to healthy communication behaviors and the one most likely to cause fights on the internet, breakups in real life, and a whole host of other problems.

In the final chapter of this first section, we'll take a look at the importance of being alone and why boredom is useful. Yes, you read that right.

**Do NOT put the book down and walk away!**

Fear of boredom is quickly becoming one of society's biggest fears, but boredom can be a seriously bad-ass catalyst for creativity. Plus, if we can't find a way to savor the act of being alone, then how will we expect anybody else to want to be with us? We need to get our shit straight before we can start working on our relationships with others, so let's go.

# 1

# MINDFULNESS IS ONLY A BUZZWORD. OR IS IT?

## Mindfulness and Presence

At this point, after taking a peek at the title to this first chapter, you might be asking yourself what the hell is mindfulness and why won't all the patchouli-smelling, granola-loving hippie people shut the fuck up about it? I suppose since I'm writing about it, that places me smack dab in the center of that stereotype, but I live in Idaho, so trust me when I state emphatically that I've been exposed to not only the influence of a healthy dosage of Pacific Northwest granola, but also an unhealthy dose of diesel fumes, so I'd like to think my approach here is reasonably balanced and targeted for nearly anyone.

Mindfulness is, at first glance, reasonably simple. It means to be aware. To be mindful means that you are aware of what's happening in the present moment.

Wow, that was surprisingly simple. Ready for Chapter 2 yet?

Hold up.

Nothing's ever that simple.

Let's see what some super smart people say about it.

Renowned clinical mindfulness researcher Jon Kabat Zinn once stated that to be mindful is to pay attention on purpose. Damn, I like that. I mean, it's so simple, but at the same time, it's really fucking profound. To "pay" means we're giving something up for something in return, while "attention" is the currency being used. Then, he added, "on purpose," which implies that we've made an intentional choice to buy into the moment using the currency of our attention. Holy shit, I could probably stop there and be totally cool with it.

But I won't. There's more.

Harvard psychologist and mindfulness researcher, Ellen Langer, suggested that being fully mindful requires four conditions to be met, and this is where shit gets real.

1. First, we must be centered in the moment, but I think we established that pretty well.
2. Second, we need to be in the moment on purpose, as Jon Kabat Zinn stated.
3. Third, we need to tap into our ability to notice that which is new in the moment, which is pretty bad-ass and something I'll explain later.
4. Finally, we have to do all this and take in everything that happens without judgment. Ouch. That's the hard part.

Let's break these down to see what mindfulness looks like in real life, at least according to the research. The first condition, obvious as it may seem, is to be centered in the present. For those unfamiliar with the lingo of hippie culture, "centered in the present" simply means we're not dwelling on something in the past, nor are we freaking the hell out about something that hasn't happened yet. It means we're focused on what's happening right here and now, and as hard as our brains may try to derail ourselves by reminding us of some bullshit someone said earlier to piss us off or some stupid-ass meeting we have to attend later in the day that could have just as easily been replaced by an email, we resist those distractions by acknowledging them and setting them aside for another time. Sounds hard already, right? Don't worry, I got us covered. We'll learn more about how to actually accomplish this through practice later on, I promise.

The second condition, as Kabat Zinn stated, is to be centered in the present *on purpose*. This means that we weren't suddenly yanked into the moment and out of our naturally distracted zombie states by noticing the awe of a pretty sunset, a really loud fucking noise, or some other unexpected assault on our other three senses. It means we've made a conscious and intentional choice to focus on what's in front of us at that moment, which also implies the decision to resist other distractions. As we'll learn later, that resistance, when noticed by others, communicates an authentic desire to spend our currency of attention on time with those in our immediate vicinity, which can be a super fucking powerful relational motivator.

The third condition, also referred to as "the confusing one" (nobody calls it that but me), means that, as we are purposefully present, we tap into an ability to notice the newness or novelty within the moment. To break this down using an example, let me tell a story. I was discussing mindfulness with a public speaking student once upon a time, and I suggested that he sit quietly, focus on his breath, and start looking at his immediate surroundings, cataloguing the various details he noticed, one bit at a time. He came back to class the following week, walked into the room before class started, and shouted, "Holy shit, Josh, that was better than drugs!" Of course, I, along with the rest of the students in the room, burst into laughter, but once we regained our composure, he explained.

The night before, my student had gone for a brief walk around the block (which becomes a separate part of a story later in this chapter, so bookmark that thought for now), and when he returned, he picked up a freshly fallen autumn maple leaf. Sitting down on his front porch, the young man started his breathing, followed by staring intently at the leaf, tracing its various veins and imagining them to be dry river beds as seen by a satellite in space. This prompted him to imagine he was some kind of benevolent god-like figure looking down on an alien planet, at which point the remaining topography of the leaf's surface began to take on new symbolic significance. Before he knew it, his father peeked out the door and asked if he was okay, to which he responded, "I'm fine, Dad, just staring at a leaf." To be honest, I'm a bit surprised his dad didn't call the school and complain after that, but the student wasn't wrong in the way he depicted this rather interesting experience.

When we make the choice to be intentionally present, we are capable of honing and refining our focus, sharpening it to a laser-like consistency, to the point where we might actually shock ourselves by the level of interesting detail all around us—detail that escapes our normal perception but becomes available once we slow our minds and allow our brains the opportunity to see things anew. Our senses, barring any exceptions, are finely tuned scientific instruments that can be manipulated to perceive things we may never have thought possible, if only we still our minds for a moment.

The fourth and final condition is by far the most difficult. Sure, we can be present, on purpose, and ready to notice all the kickass details in the moment we want, but if we can't find a way to control our tendency to place value judgments on things and experiences as they arise, then we'll doom ourselves to further mental distraction. Before we know it, we find ourselves mentally wandering off and checking out. Value judgments, by the way, are inherently valenced, which is a fancy way of saying they are always either good or bad, never indifferent. I can judge something as horrible just as easily as I can judge it by placing a positive value on it.

For example, if I'm on a walk with one of my children on a beautiful fall evening, and we stop for a moment to watch the sun disappear over beautiful Lake Coeur d'Alene, I need to be prepared to soak up that moment as fully as possible without stopping to ponder how beautiful it is. This is where shit gets tricky. It's one thing to put my arm around my daughter and watch the sun go down, *feeling* the beauty and wonder of the moment, but it's another entirely to numb my sensory perception by retreating back into my mind to *think* about how beautiful it is. The moment I stop being present and start thinking about other sunsets or other moments this reminds me of, or the moment I start composing poetry in my head that seeks to get at the essence of the moment? In either case, I've dulled my ability to absorb the details because I'm now expending mental energy on rationalizing or analyzing the moment, rather than allowing it to unfold and suspending my judgment until later.

Another example, this time on the negative valence of judgment, might be if, while on the same walk, a chilly fall breeze kicked up off the lake, and neither my daughter nor myself brought sweatshirts. My judgment of the discomfort of the wind chill could easily disrupt the magic and wonder inherent in the rest of that moment's conditions if I allow myself to latch onto that judgment. Whether positively or negatively valenced, a judgment effectively serves as a mental distraction, and the more positive or negative the value of that judgment, the more likely it can pull me out of being mindfully present.

Okay, we've got the four conditions down now, and perhaps I've made the case for why mindfulness is so important, especially given the information I dropped in the introduction, but what the hell is presence, and how does it differ from mindfulness? Think of mindfulness as a tool, like a screwdriver, a hex key (you know, an Allen wrench, better known as the tool you can never find when you need it), a hammer, and a drill. Hey, four parts to mindfulness and four tools, but we need all four to put together this goddamn Ikea mess I just unboxed in my living room. I use the tools, one at a time, taking as much care as I can as I navigate the many difficulties of such a task, and eventually, if everything goes right, I end up with a fancy Swedish end table, right? That's presence. Mindfulness provides us with the active tools, and the goal in utilizing them is to achieve and sustain presence.

## Mindlessness

Ready to go out and tackle the world yet, putting our newfound knowledge of mindfulness and presence to the test? Not yet, we aren't, so sit down. We need to talk about the polar opposite of mindfulness, and it is exactly what we'd imagine it to be called: *mindlessness*. And, no, I'm not calling anyone brainless, so don't blame me—I didn't make up the word. Mindlessness, as simply as I can possibly explain it, is the act of going through the motions. It's being on autopilot. It's giving a speech and not being able to recall what the hell you said. It's going somewhere and not remembering how you got there. It's happened to us all, and despite the bad impression the term projects, it's a necessary and important part of life.

WTF, Josh? Necessary and important? How can something called mindlessness be beneficial? Here's the deal: the human brain is a pretty fragile organ, and we know this intuitively. Physically speaking, all it takes is one good knock to the noggin for us to spend the rest of our lives as a vegetable. Not only is it a delicate and intricate part of our biological being that tends to be easily susceptible to physical damage, but when used improperly, we can actually cause damage by overloading it.

Imagine this scene for a moment. You're whipping up some boxed mac-and-cheese for lunch (or something else super simple like ramen), and something you spilled last week on the burner catches fire. You scream a few colorful, well-placed expletives (nice job, I'm proud of you) and start to panic. You remember your mom once told you something about throwing powder on a fire like that, so you start rummaging through the cabinets desperately, but you can't remember what to douse the flames with, so they grow, igniting the cabinets next. Then, the smoke alarm goes off at the same time your phone starts ringing and the kitchen is burning down. Your alarm clock goes off because your kid was screwing around with it earlier and messed it all up, but then he freaks out at the noise, flames, and smoke, and he starts screaming as well. Then the doorbell rings. It's an auditor from the IRS who wants to have a word with you, but behind him is a line that consists of vacuum salesmen, a brilliant, can't-miss, work-from-home opportunity, and someone who wants to talk with you about a personal relationship with our lord and savior. Fuck!

What I described above is essentially how it would feel like to be mindful 100% of the time. Our brains are wholly incapable of taking in all the stimuli around us at any given moment, so we prioritize our sensations and subsequent perception and interpretation of those sensory stimuli accordingly. Here's a quick and easy example with less fire and yelling. Let's say I'm driving down the interstate at 70 MPH in relatively light traffic. What am I mindful of? I'm probably paying close attention to the feel of the steering wheel, the distance between my car and those around me, the feel of the road, my position within my lane, etc. What am I ignoring? I sure as shit don't notice the design of my car's interior, the stitching of the leather, the curves of the dash, or whether it needs a dusting or not. If I did, then the next thing I'd probably become aware of is the way the guard rail feels against my car's sheet metal.

Let's get super technical. In the field of psychophysics (yes, that's a real career field filled with psychophysicists, who are not to be confused with psycho physicists or any other murderous scientists), there's a concept called the Weber-Fechner Law, which states that the way we perceive a stimulus is affected by the level of total stimuli present. That probably makes zero sense, so let's put it in context. If I'm in a dark room, and I light a candle, I most definitely notice an increase in brightness. If I light a second candle, it will double the brightness, and I'll easily notice that as well. However, if there are a hundred candles lit, and I light one more, I won't notice an increase, and I'll probably have a serious fire hazard. Simply put, if we quiet our minds and reduce distractions through mindful, intentional self-control, then we gain the ability to notice more changes and subtleties in our environment.

This is the relationship between mindfulness and mindlessness. As we grow more mindful, we become less mindless. As we get tired and need downtime, we put away the books and binge-watch our favorite Netflix series, at which point, mindlessness increases and mindfulness dwindles. This is a symbiotic relationship that is absolutely necessary, so why does mindlessness get a bad rap while mindfulness graces the cover of Time Magazine? The answer is control. Most of the time, we aren't being mindful on purpose. Instead, we act more like an impulsive toddler who bounces from one shiny distraction to the next. Acting upon impulse like this can cause us to miss out on many of life's more important moments unless they're powerful enough to pull us out of our habits. With the Age of Distraction inescapably looming, both unintentional impulses, as well as the ones manipulated by those constantly seeking our attention, continue to grow exponentially. Remember, we're talking zettabytes here.

Learning to become more mindful involves learning how to treat mindfulness and mindlessness like a light switch. If I'm at the lake with my daughter, and the sun is getting low, I can mindfully recognize the importance of that moment and put the fucking phone away to be a part of it. Then, I consciously, deliberately, and intentionally make a choice to be present for that moment, and as such, I set mindlessness aside while I exercise that part of my brain responsible for making some of the best goddamn memories a father can make.

## Developing Mindfulness

It's one thing to talk about mindfulness, mindlessness, and the need to balance both so that we can learn to take back control of our attention spans, but it's another thing to translate all this bullshit theory into a practice that actually works in our daily lives. Otherwise, this book is no better than that stupid-ass overpriced $250 calculus textbook I bought my freshman year of college before selling it back to the bookstore for $20, a pack of smokes, and a Target gift card. I lamented every torturous moment I spent with that shitty book cracked open, couldn't understand a goddamn thing in it anyway, and, like everyone else not working in a scientific, math-based field, I bitched all day long about how I'd never use that shit in the "real" world (because, you know, college is all pretend-time). I want us to be able to put this shit to use, so what we need to do is discuss realistic ways to start practicing mindfulness on a regular basis.

*Path to Mindfulness:*

- Step 1: Pull up a yoga mat. Sit on the floor.
- Step 2: Cross your legs. Place your hands on your knees, palms up, and touch your index finger to your thumb.
- Step 3: Close your eyes, breathe deeply, and hum the sound "Om" repeatedly until you feel at one with the universe.
- Step 4: Toss all those bullshit stereotypes in the garbage and move to the next paragraph. We need to work.

Don't let my sarcasm give you the wrong idea: yoga is wicked awesome, and classic meditation has its place, but that place is not here, and I couldn't teach yoga to save my damn life. What I aim to provide are practical tools that anyone can incorporate into a real person's schedule (as opposed to a fictional person who happens to be impervious to life's stressors). The activities in this chapter are designed to develop one or more of the four primary components of mindful presence: present-centered, intention, novelty, and nonjudgment. Not all these activities will work for every person; some have the potential to be profound "aha" moments for some people, while others may approach the same exercise and say, "Meh, whatevs." Some of the activities I gleefully plagiarized from ancient traditions, while some are creations of my own design that I stumbled across purely by accident. Our goal in this chapter is to try each and every one of them at least once over the period of one week. By the end of the week, I can easily guarantee that we will notice a difference, and you'll have at least a couple favorites that you'll want to continue doing regularly. Do these regularly for several weeks in a row, and the results will be life-changing.

## No Particular Place to Go

If you are reading this as a parent of school-aged children, then you will easily identify with the following story. Hell, you might identify it even as a relatively young person who knows what it's like to suffer through a summer vacation trapped in your parents' home. That stated, it was a perfect summer day at the Misner house: sunshine, no clouds, temperature in the mid-80s (that's Fahrenheit for our metric-loving Canadians, Europeans, Asians, Australians… oh hell, the rest of the world), and my four children grinding on me and my wife's raw, worn-out nerves. See, kids can only be home for so long before patience runs as thin as Gus Fring's sliced garlic, so even the slightest poorly-told but well-intentioned joke has the potential for igniting a violent firestorm. Behold, the spark with which I lit tempers aflame that day, though alas, I cannot recall for the life of me exactly what it was I said specifically. All I can state truthfully is that, as far as heated arguments go, this one would've kept us warm on a cold midwinter day. Before any lasting damage could be done, I grabbed the kids' hands and said, "Let's go."

Confused and bewildered, my kids came with me (because, you know, children are so fucking blissfully unaware of the effect their prolonged presence has upon such tempers). We walked out of the house, down the gravel driveway, and at the end, turned left. "Where are we going Daddy" they asked so innocently. "Beats me," I replied, trying to keep my cool as best as possible. I didn't tell them I was "walking it off," so to speak in hopes of avoiding saying something stupid that would get me in more trouble later on.

While my thoughts were busy ruminating—a fancy word for repeatedly replaying the entire argument in my head while saying all sorts of brilliant and witty retorts that never met the oxygen of reality—I allowed my kids to lead the way, explaining that they had total control over where we'd walk, where to turn, and even where we would end up. In reality, I was doing this so I didn't have to think about where we were going. Each time we approached an intersection, we would stop, look at one another, shrug our shoulders, and go whichever way our fancies took us. What struck me as interesting within mere minutes of embarking on this walk was how much different it felt in comparison to others from the past. Instead of power-walking with an end destination in mind, we *meandered.* Instead of rushing my kids to keep up, I found myself *letting go* of control as I let them take the lead. We stopped frequently, allowing our *attention to be captivated* by things like bugs, cracks in the sidewalk, furry squirrels roving the power lines above us, and even the strangeness of some of the street names. That's when I realized we lived near the corner of 16th and Lincoln, which is weird because Lincoln was the 16th president. Jesus, I'm a nerd. As my children led me, I noticed how liberating it felt to relinquish control. Without a firm destination in mind, I found myself *nonjudgmentally accepting* the results of letting go. Since I had nowhere to be, it made me feel like I was arriving at home with every single step.

Soon, I noticed I was no longer ruminating; I was laughing, enjoying the time we spent together, and my anger had softened up to the point where I was able to see the fight situation much more clearly. In addition to being more cognizant of my role in the argument that precipitated our walk, I started noticing much more physical detail all around my neighborhood. I even saw—*GASP*—neighbors! And we were walking by slowly enough to warrant saying hello, at which point, we stopped to talk with some of them.

After about half a mile or so, we ended up at a small soccer field. We ran all around the wide-open field, falling down occasionally in the grass as we chased butterflies and one another while playing freeze tag. As we rested in the grass, bathing in equal doses of sunshine and laughter, I noticed we were sitting in the middle of a large clover patch, so I started combing through them, hunting for the ever-elusive four-leaf clover. As I pored over the greenery, I explained to the kids the symbolism of a four-leaf clover and that roughly 1 in 10,000 clovers has a genetic mutation that produces an extra leaf, which is what makes them so desirable. At that point, my kids, who, at the time, had the attention span of a yellow lab (that's not long if you've never had one as a family pet), helped with the hunt intently, and before 15 minutes had passed, we found one four leaf clover for each of us, which might say more about all the pollutants in the water supply than our luck, but don't tell my kids that. We took our treasures home carefully, and I Pinterest-ed the shit out of those clovers into some clear epoxy so we could remember that day forever.

And it all started with a fight.

To this day, neither my wife nor myself recall the source of our contention with one another that day (except blaming it all on the kids being home for the summer – that's still true), but what we do remember is that it all started with taking a walk with no particular place to go.

## Watch What You Eat

As I watched my wife skillfully assemble an absolutely delectable Szechuan stir fry, I called my oldest daughter upstairs and invited her to sit at the dining table with me. I asked if she knew where rice came from, thinking it might be a fun little exercise before dinner, and predictably, she guessed, "Asia?" Well, yeah. I popped open the laptop and together, we looked up where rice comes from. Our search results were filled with picturesque Vietnamese and Thai rice fields, as well as a plethora of YouTube videos of people farming the crops. We perused articles on harvesting, cleaning, processing, and packaging of rice before tracing the grain's trajectory across the ocean and onto local store shelves. I then described the job of a minimum-wage stockperson, along with what it's like to ring up one customer after another and bag groceries. Before long, my teenage daughter and I had traced the entire journey of rice from seed to plate, just in time to have her dinner plate arrive in front of her.

Before she started eating, I asked her to consider all the other ingredients on her plate: red and green bell peppers, mushrooms, baby corn, snow peas, etc. Pretty soon, my daughter wasn't eating, but rather, staring at her plate quietly. I asked what was on her mind, and she told me how amazed she was at the grandiosity of the network of human effort that went into the plate sitting on the table before her. Eventually, she picked up her fork and started taking bites, but I noticed how small they were and how slowly she chewed—with intention. I could easily tell how she was concentrating on the food, thereby savoring every last nuance of her meal's individual flavors. During this meal, she maintained an ever-so-slight Mona

Lisa smile, as though it was one of the best meals she'd ever eaten. By engaging her imagination, she explored the *novelty* of thought that came with tracing the roots of her food (though I'm sure in the case of certain foods, you might want to avoid this activity – nobody wants to know the origin story behind chicken nuggets). In doing so, she slowed down and ate more *intentionally*.

A varying twist on this activity is to do the following: Before a meal, imagine it's the last food you will ever eat in your life. After all, one of these days, it will be. Depressing thoughts aside and without allowing your imagination to get too melodramatic, framing our perception of a meal in this manner forces us to slow down and activate a variety of what-if questions. It forces us to *slow down*, *dwell in the moment on purpose*, and *savor* our food much more fully, whether it's a 12-cent package of shitty chicken-flavored ramen or a perfectly seasoned ribeye. Think of it this way: Everyone has a go-to comfort food (and if you don't, you should), For me, believe it or not, it's grilled cheese sandwiches. Growing up, I often survived on these cheese-filled delights, and often, I added other ingredients to experiment, like switching processed cheese out for cheddar when we could afford to keep it around or even adding hot sauce to liven it up. It's amazing that, even when it isn't anything other than bread, butter, and cheese, the memories invoked by eating such a meal are powerful enough to encourage me to slow down and eat the sandwich mindfully, savoring every last dairy-enriched delicious morsel.

Last up, try this exercise with something as simple as a drink. I recommend coffee, but it should ideally be good coffee (I am, after all, from the Pacific Northwest, where coffee is like a religious experience), tea, cocoa, or even hot cider. Some may choose to do this with wine or other assorted adult beverages, but hey, to each their own. As we sit with our drinks, if it's hot, hold the cup in both hands, noticing the warmth. Close your eyes and pay attention to the heat as it transfers that energy to your skin and through your muscle tissue from one set of cells to another and savor the comforting sensation. Bring the cup to your nose and allow the scent to waft up and contact your olfactory nerves. Notice the smell as it begins lightly and then strengthen as the vapor intensifies. Then, place the cup close to your lips and feel the warmth there as well before taking your first sip. 'Chew' your sips, allowing the liquid to contact every last taste bud, noticing the way the flavor develops before you ingest it. As it travels your esophagus, notice the warmth you feel from the inside, smiling at the sensation. Of course, if you're doing this activity with an alcoholic beverage, repeat as necessary and take note of the warmth of your inebriation as it sets in.

Whether tracing the origin story of a pepperoni pizza, imagining your final meal that consists of a bowl of macaroni and cheese, or meditating over some warm chamomile, the point behind this exercise is to allow the experience of eating or drinking to wake you up, place you smack dab in the middle of the present moment, and afford you the opportunity to explore the novelty of your food and drink like never before.

## Seeing Red

I'd like to invoke the words of the immortal Ricky Bobby: *I wanna go fast.* I have a tendency to drive—ahem—shall we say, briskly, so when I have to slam on the brakes for a red light, especially if I need to get somewhere and have a deadline, I freely admit that I get frustrated. Okay, red lights are the fucking bane of my existence, along with people who don't know the difference between *your* and *you're* on the internet. As a result, I developed an exercise inspired by listening to a talk by the renowned Buddhist teacher, Thich Nhat Hanh, who, interestingly, was a major influence on the later work of Martin Luther King, Jr. Hanh suggested that we reframe our perception of red lights by transforming them from being an annoyance or impedance to looking at them more as a momentary relief from the chore of driving. This sounded like a challenge to me, so I decided to give it a shot.

When I initially tried this activity, I started looking around with the intention of noticing details around me, thereby exercising the skill of noticing novelty of the moment. I began noticing pedestrians so engrossed in their phones that they walked into signs or tripped over curbs. Some of the worst offenders fell flat on the sidewalk or worse, walked out into oncoming traffic. I observed other drivers, most of whom seemed to be in an imaginary staring contest with the stoplight itself, as though their glares would intimidate the light into turning green. Others picked their noses, performed serenades with their windows rolled up, or seemed to stare intently at their crotches until it was time to go again.

The more I did this activity, the more entertaining it became, so I decided to crank it up a notch, and that's when I began imagining stories about the people I observed. The lady in the BMW with the dark tinted windows invented Post-Its. The guy in the jacked-up truck with the monster tires was a Russian secret agent who knew the perfect cover to blend into a northern Idaho environment. The elderly couple sneaking a kiss in the car behind me was celebrating their 75th anniversary. Regardless of the outcome of each story, I began to look forward to the next red light. I developed an anticipation that transformed my interpretation of the hassle of stopping my commute into a fun and refreshing activity. I ended up getting to work at the exact same time, too, so despite all my complaints about being stopped at punishment lights (thanks for the term, Nancy Botwin), it was all a perception of my own making.

## Out-Smartphone

If you recall the introduction, I briefly discussed the infamous torturer of rodents, B.F. Skinner, whose discovery of the intricacies of operant conditioning showed us how obsessive and compulsive behaviors develop, along with Pavlov, whose experiments with dogs and the dinner bell further showed us how this conditioning can totally fuck us up. That conditioning short circuits our brain's chemical reward system so easily that, when manipulated, we usually don't notice it happening. The one major characteristic we humans share with rats and dogs is that we are animals with the same basic reward systems, but instead of satisfying a craving for food, we're looking at our need for social interaction.

Recent academic studies have shown that social isolation has a comparable mortality rate to that of smoking, meaning that, in the end, loneliness really can kill a person—not figuratively—but it can actually cause a person to no longer exist in a slow, painful process of deterioration. Is that some shit or what? It is an imperative of biology for us to seek out that social interaction, as it is hardwired straight into our DNA. As such, it probably shouldn't surprise us that we get a chemical high from positive social interaction. Think about this: If I sign up for a social media account like Facebook, and I quickly learn that it works by posting things for my "friends" to "like" and, as a result, I get a notification by way of an audible ding, a vibration on my phone, and that stupid little red number sitting on the app's icon. Those stimuli (audio, tactile, and visual) all quickly become associated with the tiny dopamine boost I get from knowing one of my "friends" positively reinforced what I shared. Within days or potentially even less time, I am quickly conditioned to automatically and mindlessly grab my phone and see who liked what I shared every fucking time one of those notifications goes off. Some of us may even drool like Pavlov's dog, but that's another issue for another book.

The next time you experience one of these notifications, whether from social media, email, a phone call, a text, or any other app, pay close attention to the amount of time that elapses from the moment you recognize the notification to the moment you're reaching for the phone. If you're anything like me or the rest of our doomed species, I'm willing to bet there's not a lot of time that elapses. Much like the dog in the Pixar film, *Up*, we are easily conditioned to become slaves to these impulses, almost like having an electronic squirrel in our pockets.

Similar to our red light activity, we need to reframe the situation and reprogram ourselves to take back control over our attention. The moment we receive and recognize the notification, whether hearing a ding, feeling a buzz, or perhaps simply seeing the screen light up, we need to use those stimuli as triggers to *pause* instead of mindlessly grab for the device. When it goes off, stop and take 1-2 deep, cleansing breaths. Without looking at the device, ponder who might be trying to contact you and why. Take your time before grasping the phone and seeing who the notification is from, but even as you do, imagine what that person is doing at the moment. Even if the person on the other end of the communique is a call center worker in Mumbai, think about that person's day. How many irate Americans do you think that person dealt with in her underpaid and outsourced position before calling you? Eventually, you will need to examine the source of the notification, but do so only after clearing your mind and putting yourself into a frame of thought that is open and *free from judgment* of the situation. One of the most immediate benefits to this exercise you will notice is a satisfying feeling of control, as well as feeling pride at resisting this programmable sense of urgency.

Think about it. You are taking control over your entrance and exit with respect to the world of electronic communication.

You are a fucking boss. Own that shit.

## Why the Hell Should We Care?

Over the course of this chapter, we've discussed the definitions of mindfulness and mindlessness, and we've explored a variety of activities we can employ on a regular basis to help develop these behaviors, thereby reclaiming control of our attention and doing so with a renewed sense of purpose. We now know that each of these activities addresses a specific component within the four major building blocks to mindful presence:

- Going for a walk or even a drive with no destination in mind gives us the opportunity to develop greater situational awareness, but it also challenges ourselves to let go of the need to think more about a destination than the present in which we inhabit.
- Eating and/or drinking mindfully teaches us to slow down and savor, which you probably already know is a well-established method to reduce portion size, since it takes about 20 minutes for our brains to realize we're full. Consuming sustenance deliberately also brings significantly more enjoyment to eating and drinking, and imagining the route our food took to get to our plates can give us a greater appreciation for not only the food or drink, but also the network of human interaction that made it happen.
- The stoplight activity can greatly reduce a major source of stress and also helps us practice the art of intentionally reshaping perceptions, transforming potentially irritating situations into something to which we may actually look forward.
- Retraining ourselves to stop and collect our thoughts before looking at a device notification reclaims control over where we direct our attention, thereby fighting back against operant

conditioning. Additionally, this brief moment can also frame our moods appropriately before interacting with others.

### Chapter Challenge: Wake Up!

Guess what? Your task now is to go out and try each one of these activities over the course of one week. I recommend trying them on different days so you have the opportunity at the end of the day to look back on the activities and more accurately assess the impact they had on your mood. As mentioned, not all of these activities will produce a mind-blowing experience. For some people, like my student who claimed the exercises were better than drugs, the exercises were pretty fucking profound, but don't go into the activities expecting something. Instead, practice the quality of remaining nonjudgmental so you can experience the effects as fully and objectively as possible. In most cases, the activities are much more likely to produce subtle and incremental changes that add up over time, particularly changes to stress, anxiety, depression, and a more heightened sense of self-awareness.

Also, consider adding your own creative spin on the activities! Ask yourself the following question: Where do your best ideas happen? Arguing with yourself in the shower? Taking the Browns to the Super Bowl? Doing the dishes? Folding the laundry? All these activities have something in common with the activities I proposed in this chapter. All are simple, menial chores that require a small amount of concentration but little to no thought, which allows our minds to quiet down, set aside distraction, and work much more efficiently. There's nothing wrong with "dish meditation" or "deuce-dropping mediation" if that works for you. For some people cooking is their meditation, so if that's you, go with the flow.

But none of this is possible until we put the fucking phone down, so let's practice mindfulness together . . .

As you complete each one, be sure to set aside time at the end of your day to reflect on how each activity impacted your daily routine. I highly encourage you to write down your thoughts. Writing them down, as you will do in later activities as well, puts everything in one spot and makes it easier to refer back to later. Here's a few thought-provoking questions to get your creative blood flowing:

We know that the difference between going through the motions, acting on autopilot, and being mindless is far different than being mindfully present, particularly when it comes to interacting with people close to us. Think about people in your life who exemplify presence. How do they make you feel when you are around them? What qualities do they display that make you feel like they are great examples of mindfulness?

Think about times when you were mindfully present. How did it feel for you to allow the rest of the world to disappear as you lost yourself within the intricacies of that moment?

At the conclusion of the week, which of the activities seemed to have the most impact? Did any of them seem to build off of one another, or did one individual activity seem more effective than all the others? How will you incorporate these activities in future weeks, even as we move beyond this chapter?

Think back to some of your favorite memories of time spent with loved ones. As you sample a few, try to identify the role mindful presence played in those moments. Did you make a conscious decision to be present, or did it happen more naturally? Do you think you can control your presence to facilitate more of these moments in the future?

# 2

# WE ALL WANT TO BE HEARD. TOO BAD NOBODY WANTS TO LISTEN.

I swear, I can hear your thoughts, even as I type this out: "Great, a sanctimonious, self-important asshole telling me I'm not listening, just like my mother/father/spouse/partner/fill-in-the-blank." You're partly right; I'm sure I can be an asshole sometimes (my wife will vouch). Also, you're probably not listening enough, but it's not (completely) your fault. We all have a butt-load of room to improve when it comes to listening, so put down the pitchfork and torch and stand down. Remember that I'm partially writing this book as a reminder to myself to stop being such a dick, and if I'm being vulnerable here, I'll admit that listening is my kryptonite.

Perhaps the next thought is, "Okay, so if you suck at listening, then why should I believe you?" It's not that I suck at listening. The problem is that I have a good 30 years or so of shitty habits to undo. That doesn't happen overnight, so I've spent the last 15 years trying to unravel the tangled web I wove. And, if I have shitty habits that I picked up from sources like, oh, I don't know, LIFE, then odds are, the rest of us probably picked up a few as well without knowing. No matter what type of listener I *think* I might be because so-and-so once feigned on and on about what a marvelous listener I was after sitting through an epic, traumatic breakup saga when in reality, I slept through their melodrama with my eyes open, then this chapter is not only directed toward me, but also anyone else in the same boat.

### Listening 101

Whether you were raised in Idaho or Iowa, Washington State or D.C., or Florida or … um … France, there isn't an educational system in the world that treats listening with the same priority as other aspects of interaction. Some school systems don't even stress the importance of oral communication in general. I should know because I was part of one of those systems as a kid. In fact, I didn't give my first formal speech until I was a 28-year-old college freshman who thought it was insanely fucking stupid that I was being forced to give a speech when I planned on going into research physics anyway. Then again, look at me now. Looks like that class made an impact.

So, why don't we treat listening with more respect when it comes to learning more about it? I mean, we all know the difference between hearing and listening, right? Hearing is a passive activity that everyone within hearing culture (i.e., not hearing impaired or deaf) can do without effort. Eardrums vibrate, sending electrical impulses to the brain, and the mind recognizes that as sound. Listening, on the other hand, requires *effort*, and that's where the differences begin. Knowing that it requires effort also implies that some of us do it well while others do not. In 55 A.D., a philosopher dude by the name of Epictetus said, "We have two ears and one mouth so that we can listen twice as much as we speak." Moments later, his wife snickered. Just kidding, he lived alone for most of his life, so he probably didn't get a chance to really experience married life.

Even beyond the whole hearing thing, those within the deaf world also listen, but they do so with their eyes instead. Listening isn't confined to the domain of one's ears; listening is also an observational activity that includes paying attention to one's nonverbal communication signals. In that regard, listening can be thought of as: *the act of placing mental effort on the perception, selection, and interpretation of messages using one or more of our senses.* At least, that's the operational definition we're running with for the rest of this book. In other words, listening involves paying attention to not only what's being said, but how it's being said and equally important — what's not being said.

Becoming a great listener requires a hefty fuck-ton of commitment, so if we aren't prepared to devote the necessary time and energy, then we might as well stop here because everything else in this book depends upon committing to the pursuit of active, mindful listening skills. As you will soon learn, certain types of listening definitely require more effort than others, especially if we're going to learn to put our fucking phones down and start practicing the art of listening to others. Of the various styles I describe, most should sound pretty familiar, although most of us tend to gravitate toward one or two primary styles, depending on the situation. The trick lies in our ability to actively discern which style is required based on the needs of the situation and then make a conscious, deliberate, and intentional choice to switch to that style.

### Damaging Styles

Look, I'm a big fan of villains, the dark side, and diving into the bad news first, so let's start there. Two styles of listening—defensive and superficial—have abso-fucking-lutely no place in human interaction. Their presence alone predicts, with surprising accuracy, oncoming conflict with superior regularity, all while highlighting some fairly serious personal issues. While it's ridiculously easy for me to enjoy the view up here from my high horse and tell you not to use either style, it's unfortunately easier said than done.

### *Defensive Listening*

Defensive listening is undoubtedly the most harmful fucking style of listening. It requires little to no cognitive effort, being primarily emotion-driven and reactive by its nature. The main focus for this style of listening is—wait for it—the self! Surprised? People who gravitate toward defensive listening strut around with precariously balanced shoulder chips the size of Madagascar; everything and anything is clearly an ominous threat to their fragile egos, and when these threats become imminent, defensive listeners melt down like cotton candy in a toddler's sticky-ass, saliva-soaked fingers. Such chips act as hot buttons or triggers that, regardless of others' intent, cause defensive listeners to recklessly abandon every last remaining fragment of their shit, often in spectacular fashion.

I have a confession to make: I was one of these people at one time in my life. From the earliest time I can remember, I felt insecure and insignificant. Perhaps it had to do with not hitting a significant growth spurt until my freshman year of high school, at the start of which I measured a tad shorter than five feet (though I would later grow another 10 inches in only a couple of years). It may have been the result of harboring the impression that I couldn't please or impress my parents. It could have been the result of all this, combined with the lovely chemical imbalance that comes with puberty. Who the fuck knows?

Regardless, I was a certified grade-A dick most of the time. Being right was far more important than being loved, and I wore my arrogance like a fucking badge. Even when I wasn't right, I tried to find a way into arguing that I was, even when that meant changing the subject or trying to make the other person feel like shit for being right. I was a master of what's called *kitchen sinking*, or the act of digging up wholly irrelevant disagreements, annoyances, or inconsistencies from the distant past, and then rubbing my opponent's face in them like a dog who just shit the rug. I viewed arguments as contests to be won at any cost, even if winning meant losing a relationship, because, in my insecure brain, being right felt better than being loved. Holy Jesus' sacred man-tits, that was painful to type.

I'm feeling much better now, and in a future chapter, I'll dish the dirt on exactly what turned me around (spoiler alert: my wife is a bad-ass).

Some of us aren't naturally defensive listeners like this; some of us accidentally step in defensiveness like wandering around the back yard in the fall, knowing full well all the squishy surprises the dogs left behind to discover lurking beneath the leaf carpet. This often happens during moments of HALT: Hungry, Angry, Lonely, or Tired. Other times, it might surface unexpectedly because we're hauling around a bunch of unresolved emotional baggage like a briefcase chained to our wrists, and when someone says something hurtful that causes our personal suitcase to suddenly rupture, we unintentionally project that pain onto others and fail to realize what we've done until it's time to apologize.

Defensiveness is an irrational and volatile act, almost completely devoid of reason. I often like to think of reacting defensively as being a situation where I've got an angel on one shoulder saying, "Bruh, don't say tha… Aw, shit, you said it." On the other side, the little devil has full control over the mic, and it's show time. It's hard to stop ourselves when we get like this. It's difficult to listen to the little angel instead of the devil who has a remarkably deft talent for persuasion. In cases of a person who walks around like a raw, exposed nerve like I used to do, there isn't one cute little fucking cherub to be found—only the empty footprints where he stood before the devil kicked his ass and duct-taped him to a chair.

*Superficial Listening*

The other type of harmful listening—superficial listening—is like the light beer of harmful listening behaviors. A little now and then probably isn't all that bad for you, but enough of it ends up making you feel like shit the next morning. Superficial listening is exactly what it sounds like; it means you've checked right the fuck out, and you aren't returning anytime soon. This style of listening typically kicks in when we're bored AF. It can also happen when there's something far more interesting, entertaining, or important happening inside our heads. For example, if a student comes to me with a trivial or minor annoyance, and I have only five minutes to get to a meeting, there's a good chance I'm thinking more about my punctuality than their issues. This isn't to say I actually do this, because in all honesty, fuck meetings. Meetings are the bane of my goddamn existence, especially when we all could have saved an hour with one or two well-crafted emails. I could be doing so much more with my time. Would you look at that? I'm totally demonstrating superficial listening as you read this. See how that works?

Superficial listening normally only harms the person doing it, like when a student checks out during class and ends up failing the midterm. Think of superficial listening within more important contexts, and it's not difficult to imagine this behavior harming not only our relationships but also other people in a real and tangible form, especially when the allure of a fucking phone is involved. Think of a doctor checking out of a conversation as her patient describes the symptoms of a mystery illness. Imagine a husband spacing off as his partner explains what's wrong with their relationship. Picture a child staring out the window as his him what time he needs to be home—or else. These situation potential hazards—not only to the person who isn't being fu but also the person not being listened to.

Aside from placing individuals at risk, superficial listening also jeopardizes our interpersonal relationships. Remember when, only a few paragraphs ago, I mentioned how much of a defensive ass I used to be (and still can be, I'm sure), only to have one specific situation act as the catalyst that changed it all? The same story applies here. Ultimately, it was a superficial listening situation that caused a friend to call me out, at which point, my wife stepped in to finish the job by pointing out my defensive tendencies. I genuinely anticipate with baited glee being able to dish the dirt and share this story, but I'm afraid it has to wait until Chapter 4, so keep reading.

Superficial listening requires absolutely no fucking effort; in fact, that's the root of the problem. We listen superficially not only when we're bored AF, but we also do it when we're tired AF. As mentioned previously, listening is an active process, and the energy required to do so increases with the level of engagement desired. By the power of deduction, if there's zero effort, there's also zero engagement. Think of superficial listening as distracted listening, and with this in mind, perhaps it isn't always an issue of being unmotivated, but it could also happen if we get distracted by someone's hair, a stain on their shirt, an offensive or hilarious message on a hat or shirt, etc.

SQUIRREL!

Ultimately, superficial listening occurs when something causes us to check out of the present moment and retreat elsewhere (*ahem* PHONES), regardless of whether our attention spans are kicking back in the imaginary leather recliner of our minds, or we're suddenly reminiscing about that one time at band camp. Superficial listening may not carry as many harmful side effects as defensive listening, but it sure as shit doesn't present any positive benefits.

### Listening Styles that Get Shit Done

With the dark side out of the way, we can now turn our attention to listening styles that actually have benefits, and if we can ever pull ourselves away from those tiny fucking screens, maybe we can practice using these and learn more about the people involved in our lives. Often called 'task-focused' listening styles, these four types of listening—detailed, comprehensive, persuasive, and analytical listening—are employed for various purposes, but each carries a clear focus and should be used appropriately. Choosing the wrong one that ignores the needs of a situation can easily backfire and result in a seriously shitty outcome, so it's important for us to recognize the characteristics of each and know how to wield them differently. Think of the mind like the shifter in a car with a manual transmission. If you need to back out of a parking space at the grocery store, you'll probably use reverse, because if not, you'll get to know your insurance agent pretty fucking well over the next few weeks, not to mention probably cash in all your favors with friends to be able to get to school or work. Knowing the right listening style and choosing one consciously and deliberately is like shifting gears in your mind, so let's pop the clutch on this baby and get moving.

*Detailed Listening*

First up in the task-focused listening category is a style that I am notoriously horrible at using, and I'll share a little story with you in a bit to illustrate why. Detailed listening is like listening on a mission, where you listen for highly specific information. If you're starting your first day on a new job, and someone needs to train you to input data into an unfamiliar computer system or how to use a cash register, then you're paying attention to the details you need to function at that task. If your child or partner calls you, asking you to pick up a few things at the store on the way home from work, you're listening to the list and trying to save that information for later. Students tend to be mostly proficient at this style, especially if a teacher announces, "This will be on the final . . ." moments before speaking. The drawback and potential pitfall of this listening style is that listeners are so busy gathering and memorizing details that they fail to assemble it to see the bigger picture. Students, like those in our example, might be able to memorize and regurgitate certain facts and figures, but when asked to provide a synthesis or analysis on exactly what those facts and figures mean in a bigger sense, they find themselves giving the classic 1000-yard stare.

*Comprehensive Listening*

Where detailed listening is concerned with expending listening energy on capturing the minutiae of details and ordered steps, we can think of comprehensive listening as exactly the fucking opposite. People who are naturally drawn toward comprehensive listening, such as yours truly, tend to be much more concerned with how everything fits together and what it means in a deep, existential sense of our understanding of the meaning of life or some shit. Given the fact that I've been teaching public speaking since 2008, it's become something of a habit. Like, no shit, if I'm watching broadcast television (which isn't often), and I have to suffer through a commercial break with more than 2-3 ads, I'm piecing together where the money comes from to support the station, the show, and what messages they're trying to indoctrinate us all to believe. It's really goddamn annoying.

But if you want to hear just how annoying such a habit can be, few of my stories illustrate it better than the one I've been saving up since I discussed detailed listening only a few pages ago. Long ago, well before I had ever learned more about my listening tendencies and use of different styles based on situational needs, I had the opportunity to suddenly become highly self-aware of my listening shortcomings.

It was a family shopping day, the kind you dread as a parent, where one has to hit Costco and at least two other stores for a big shopping trip—with two kids in tow. As per their usual, my kids grew impatient and started acting up (AKA, being miniature assholes) about halfway through the second store, so by the time we got to the last grocery store, my wife had enough, and I was well on the express bus to downtown crazy-town. She said, "You go in, since we only need three things. I don't want to end up murdering our children." Admit it, fellow parents. You've been there.

My wife told me the three items, and I started across the parking lot, feeling relieved to be alone and outside the car in the relative silence and peace while she stayed behind with my little devil children. As I walked, I suddenly noticed that all three items began with the letter P, which mildly amused me.

*Huh, three Ps*, I thought.

By the moment when I walked through the door to the store, that's all I could fucking remember.

I frantically searched my memory for the three items, naming off everything we usually purchase that started with P, but alas, I couldn't recall what they were. Now, a bit of backstory, my wife always makes fun of my short-term memory. I can remember every address, every phone number, and even the goddamn VIN number to my first car. But give me three stupid fucking things to remember, and I've forgotten them 30 seconds later.

That stated, I didn't want to give her the pleasure of being right yet again. I could've easily texted her and asked for the three items again, but I would've never heard the fucking end of it, so I walked up and down each aisle of the store, grabbing everything I could that began with P. I grabbed: popcorn, peanuts, pistachios, parmesan, pickles, prosciutto, pepperoni, pastrami, and paper towels. I had: a papaya, a pineapple, a stack of post-it notes, and a package of pens. By the time I was done, I had more than 30 items and probably spent way more money than I should have, but in my fragile male ego, I was avoiding ridicule, so it was a justified cost.

I walked to the car triumphantly, almost skipping as I walked, were it not for the sheer weight of my grocery haul, knowing there was no way she would find me out. I handed the bags to her as I got in, and she looked at them curiously. A bead of sweat formed on my brow, but I avoided eye contact. I couldn't let on that I was nervous. She dug through the bags as I pulled out of our parking spot but then stopped abruptly.

"Josh?"

"Yes, dear?"

"Where's my pop?"

"Uh . . ."

"You forgot, didn't you?"

"Um, no! I just got some extra stuff that I thought we might need for, uh . . ."

"How is it that you left the store with four goddamn bags of shit that all starts with P and yet, somehow, you still forgot all three of the things I asked for?"

I froze. "Fuck."

"That's what I thought." Stacie: 1. Josh: 0.

Turns out, I have a pretty great grasp on comprehensive listening. After all, that's part of my job as a communication professor. I need to be able to extract overall messages from speeches and other forms of communication. Unfortunately, I didn't know how to shut that shit down and shift gears so that I was tapping into a different listening style, one that was better suited to the needs of the situation, and as a result, I now have a story to tell and a reputation I can't shake. Every last student who has heard this story not only nearly passes out from laughing, but then, when they see me in public later on, they'll ask if I have a grocery list or not. Little bastards.

Of course, now that I know my listening tendencies, whenever I need a list of details, such as when going shopping, my wife knows to text me an actual list.

But, to this day, I don't recall what those three items were.

And my wife refuses to tell me.

### *Persuasive Listening*

We can think of the persuasive listening as a more elevated or nuanced version of detailed listening with elements of comprehensive listening thrown for good measure. Picture an automotive salesperson listening to customers talk about their wants and needs, gathering details and reassembling those into a potential solution that not only makes the customers happy, but also provides a living for that salesperson's family through a reasonable commission. There's a bit more effort involved in this style as opposed to either detailed or comprehensive listening alone, and if you're using this style as the basis to earn a living, then I have quite a bit of respect for you, because that sounds like hard goddamn work.

*Analytical Listening*

Of the big four "get shit done" listening styles, this one is the hardest to do because it requires the most cognitive energy, by far. Obviously, applying so much energy to listening has its drawbacks, because we can only do it for so long before it ends up making us feel absolutely fucking drained and exhausted. This style is most often employed by debate competitors or, if they're particularly skilled at their art form, we might refer to them as *master debaters*. Good lord, I am a child.

Anyone running for public office and planning on participating in town hall meetings or public debates might do well to learn to use this style skillfully. Analytical listening requires one to resist all distractions and focus solely on the message of the other speaker, but it also necessitates keeping one's emotions in check, avoiding judgment or hasty conclusions, and using what's called the *thought-speech-time differential*, or the quiet milliseconds between what things being said, to mentally piece together the message and analyze not only its pieces but how it fits together as a whole. See, we think at a rate of around 400-500 words per minute, but we only talk at about 150 words per minute, so that gives us a good bit of time to allow our brains to analyze while others flap their yappers.

Skilled analytical listeners are not only amazing at listening and analysis but frequently are also adept at crafting a carefully thought-out response. These listeners, however, are vulnerable to a relatively common isotope of kryptonite: holes in logic or reasoning. When things don't add up as rationally as they should, an analytical listener easily derails while considering all possible refutations to the error. Analytical listening obviously takes practice, as well as training because, to analyze accurately, one has to study argumentation as a science and art form, but with enough development, one can certainly become a certified bad-ass.

## People-Focused Listening Styles

Now that we've covered the four task-focused (or get-shit-done) listening styles, let's take a look at the styles we should utilize when we're not as concerned with the task at hand but instead, those styles we want to use when we're more invested in developing and nurturing connection with others. Not everything can be about completing tasks or solving problems. Some interactions require a more compassionate and relational ear. Guys, are you paying attention? Yes, I'm writing this specifically for men (myself included), as it is one of the hardest things in the world for a typical man to perform, given the way we're socialized, as well as how our brains are wired biologically. With this genre of listening, there's only two styles to discuss, but even though there's fewer styles, they make up for quantity in terms of complexity.

### *Relational Listening*

Remember persuasive listening? Of course, you fucking do. That was literally like three paragraphs ago. Plus, it also starts with P. If you don't remember it, we have some pretty serious issues to discuss. Relational listening is almost the same as persuasive listening, but where the persuasive style listens for specific details to be used later as a means to motivate, persuade, or inspire others, relational listening pays attention to details that can then be connected or related to something else. For example, during the first week or so of every semester in my intro to public speaking class, where I have a room full of 20 or so terrified students, all of whom are petrified at the idea of getting up in front of me and their peers to speak, I have each person do a "warm-up" speech, where they stand up for about a minute and introduce themselves. During that introduction, I listen carefully and write down details from their individual stories that have some sort of connection to me and my life story. After all the students are finished, I then walk around the room, stopping at each person, and explaining how they're connected to me, which sounds something like this:

*"Oh, you play basketball? Yeah, I did too, until a knee injury took me out of the game."*

*"You grew up in a shitty neighborhood in Seattle? Wow, my childhood neighborhood was called Felony Flats!"*

*"You live on a ranch and take care of cattle? That's so cool! My son's spirit animal is a cow! We're hoping to get him one someday."*

By doing this with each and every student, it not only makes them feel as though they are seen and heard as individuals, but it puts them more at ease by knowing more about the intricate web of connections we have that relate every one of us to each other.

Most of us won't end up communication professors though (thankfully), so where else might this style be useful? Um, DUH! How about married life, particularly during the newlywed phase? It is so un-fucking-believably important for young couples to learn to observe one another and listen for these connections. The more they relate to one another, the stronger the relationship becomes in the long run. However, this is true for nearly every type of relationship: friends, in-laws, extended family, and hell, even coworkers! We humans have such a strong natural desire to connect with one another, so it makes sense to do this early in any relationship as a means to deepen and strengthen those bonds.

### *Mindful Listening*

All predictability aside with saving the one called 'mindful listening' for last, this is the style of listening I personally find more important than any other, and unsurprisingly, it's one of the hardest styles to perfect as a skill. Mindful listening requires the most mental effort, but more than that, it also requires the most acute focus on others. Essentially, this is the people-focused version of analytical listening as explained earlier. Mindful listening, despite its highly rewarding nature, is also emotionally draining in much the same way that analytical listening is mentally draining.

Just as the analytical listener shifts the gears of the mind to pay attention to and analyze details, the mindful listener must be prepared to fully and wholly empathize with the other person, mirroring their emotional state as a means to develop a deep understanding. There are five steps one can employ to practice the art of mindful listening:

- First, bring your attention to your breath. Notice the air moving in through your nose and down your esophagus and then notice how it feels to exhale. Breathe slowly and deliberately, clearing the mind of all external distractions. Doing this early on helps quiet the mind, but it's not a meditation session, so resist the temptation to start doing yoga.
- Second, focus on nonverbal cues that tell the other person we are actively engaged in the conversation, such as maintaining eye contact, nodding the head, leaning toward the speaker rather than away, opening up our stance rather than closing off by crossing the arms, facing the other person directly, and being conscious of how the other person might interpret our facial expressions.
- Third, imagine you are a mirror. Using your nonverbal communication, mirror the other speaker, though take care not to make it painfully obvious. This helps to activate the mirror neurons in both your brain and the other person's brain, creating a neural pathway for relating to take place. Wait for breaks in the conversation to reflect and relate the speaker's message back to her or him.
- Fourth, seek clarification as needed. Analyze the content of the message to ensure full understanding, and ask follow-up questions to seek further detail for greater understanding. This is not done to interrogate, so don't be an asshole about it.
- Fifth and most importantly, engage in a bit of perception checking. Occasionally, as you reflect back to the speaker, check in to make sure what you've heard is understood as the other person originally intended. For example, "If I understand you correctly, you're saying that I've been a little bitch lately and need to withdraw my head from my ass?" Remember that this step, like seeking clarification, is done from a place of nonjudgment (hence, the mindful designation), so the hardest part is in resisting the distraction of defensiveness, particularly if the other person is sharing something frustrating related to yourself.

An important piece of advice for anyone seeking to practice mindful listening: Take care of yourself. Mindful listening can be a miracle worker when we apply it to someone going through some seriously nasty life-shit, but it opens up an emotional conduit between you and that person, effectively causing you to experience a taste of it as well. Not only can that be draining, but if you're particularly well-suited or inclined to experience empathy, that means you may end up feeling what the other person feels. If that mess goes down, you need to take a good, long timeout to unwind and deal with that shit or else their baggage becomes yours. You don't want to carry around anymore than you already have.

## The Listening Toolbox

As cliché as it may seem, all of these listening styles are merely tools within a larger set. Of course, defensive and superficial listening represent those shitty, useless tools that your officemate bought for you that one Christmas when they drew your name in the secret Santa pool and ended up getting you one of those $19.99 as-seen-on-TV tools hocked by the really creepy, shouty guy with spiky hair and permanently dilated pupils. It's the gift nobody wants with a price tag not quite high enough to warrant a trip to Target to face the post-holiday return line. The other styles, however, represent tools that really *are* useful, like a classic flathead screwdriver or the half-inch socket that always goes missing right when you need it most. As with hand tools, these listening tools have a place and time. As demonstrated in the story of the three Ps, using the wrong style for the needs of the situation results in one or more components of the basic communication model going wrong. Once one component breaks down, miscommunication has taken place, and when that happens, the consequences can be disastrous.

We all engage in each of these styles at various points and times, and we all gravitate toward one or two specific styles based on our personalities and life histories. Mine used to be defensive listening, but as soon as I became aware and made the conscious choice to eliminate that style from my repertoire, comprehensive became my primary style. Taking the time to watch and reflect on how we listen can provide the insight we need to take control over the gears we shift our minds into, and doing so can radically change the outcomes of our interactions.

For example, if my wife gives me a grocery list, then that's my cue to shift into detailed listening. If you're sitting in a classroom, studying philosophy, that's a great time to deploy your comprehensive listening style, but if you're studying math or science, you may want to switch gears to analytical listening. If a good friend comes to you, dejected, despondent, and in desperate need of a supportive ear, recognize that you may need to shift to mindful listening and use it to ease that friend's suffering. Being mindful enough to discern the needs of the moment and then *choose* the listening style most apropos to that moment is a skill developed over time and with conscious effort.

But none of that is going to happen until we agree to put our fucking phones down, so here's a chapter challenge to put this shit into practice:

### Chapter Challenge: The Last Word

For this challenge, select a person close to you or someone you'd like to be closer to you, and seek out a chance to have an extended conversation. Don't force it, and don't overthink it. Simply remain vigilant, and watch for the opportunity to present itself. Once the conversation starts, deploy your imagination and tell yourself that this could be the last conversation you'll ever have with that person because that person is going to die in a tragic accident shortly after you're done. Okay, scratch that. Don't go that far. This isn't method acting, so there's no need to pursue a daytime Emmy, but you get the idea; approach this time as though you'll never get another chance to relive it. Hang on each and every word, and treat each thought the other person shares with you as though it was an incredibly fragile, delicate, and priceless trinket by handling it and admiring it with care. If the conversation slows down, ask clarifying questions, ask why/what/who/when/where/how to keep them talking, and as you do, focus on demonstrating sincere interest. As this scene unfolds, pay close attention to how your time with this person feels different than interactions in the past.

Allow your time together to go on as long as needed. Don't rush, don't worry about the time, and allow yourself to surrender to the beauty of this moment. After it's over and done with, as soon as possible, journal your thoughts. Contemplate what happened by unpacking how the simple act of framing your approach to the conversation changed the way you perceived it. Try to identify which listening styles you use and how well they worked. Analyze how you felt after the conversation, in terms of energy; were you a bit drained and tired, or were you energized?

# 3

## BORED? SUCK IT UP, BUTTERCUP.

Let's kick off this chapter with a series of thought experiments. Read through the following paragraphs slowly and deliberately, trying to imagine yourself in each situation, culminating in the question, what would you do?

You've arrived at the grocery store, and you only need to get a couple of things, maybe a gallon of milk (almond milk if you're vegan) and a delicious sauvignon blanc (or a fine vintage of iced tea if you don't imbibe). Two items in hand, you head to the register, only to find that every last fucking lane is at least 4-5 people deep, so you make your way to the express lane, hoping it moves a tad faster. However, the customer at this register apparently can't read the giant "12 Items or Less" sign above the register, so it's going to be a while. You sigh in frustration and accept your fate. What do you do?

You've arrived at your child's school to pick her or him up (or perhaps your little brother or sister because you're such an amazing person who helps your parents out by picking up siblings from school), and you're a little early. You glance at the clock tower on the church across the street and realize you have 15 minutes to wait, but that's okay, because it's sunny and warm. Copping a squat on the granite stone outside the school doors, you notice other parents or (super helpful) older siblings as they show up, but nobody makes eye contact with anyone else. Instead, they all pull out their fucking phones and endlessly scroll. What do you do?

It's time for your annual physical, so you make an appointment with your family doctor. Upon arrival, you sign in, pay your obnoxiously expensive copay and think about moving to Canada before the receptionist directs you to have a seat, but then mentions they're running a bit behind, so you may have to wait longer than normal. He apologizes, so you take your seat in the crowded waiting room. There's a little boy, probably two years old or so, playing nearby, and he keeps staring at you, reaching the depths of your soul with his piercing, creepy gaze. You smile and wave, and he goes about his business with a set of blocks. Looking around the waiting room, you notice everyone else is on their fucking phones, and none of the magazines look even remotely interesting. What do you do?

I'm assuming with relative accuracy that I can predict what you all would have done next, and it's probably pretty fucking unlikely that I know you. If you're anything like me or any other person in the developed world who owns a mobile device that connects us to the rest of humanity, then you probably would have, without thinking, whipped out your phone and busied your mind with something – *anything.* If your answer was anything but the option of checking your phone, playing some mindless time-burner of a game, or scrolling your news feed endlessly while you waited, then you're probably lying to yourself. It's time for us to face it: We ALL do this. We see it happening all around us nearly every moment of every day.

We live in an *impatient space.* What I mean by this term is that, as life slows down, we seem to have a natural and conditioned response to that impending quiet, which propels us toward seeking the next thing to occupy our attention. I've used an activity in my classrooms before, where I tell my class that we're going to spend three minutes in complete silence. Nobody can close their eyes and sleep through the three minutes, nor can they busy themselves by reading or scrolling. Instead, we simply sit in silence together for a full three minutes. You should see their eyes when I announce this. I may as well announce that our guest speaker for the day is a greasy, stank-ass hillbilly with a chainsaw and a mask made from the skin of his prior victims. In fact, such a guest "lecture" may be preferable for many.

During this time, people behave predictably. The first 30 seconds are the easiest. From 30-45 seconds, everyone contracts a case of the giggles, and students try to stifle themselves. After the one-minute mark, eyes wander, desperately seeking *something* to occupy their attention. Some count ceiling tiles, others stare out the window at cloud formations, and many discover solace in examining feet. From 90 seconds to the two-minute mark, students visibly squirm in their seats like a crack addict jonesing for a fix, but once we get into the second minute, something remarkable happens.

People chill the fuck out. They no longer avoid eye contact with me or one another. They smile quaint little grins. The squirming subsides, they sit up a bit straighter, and the tension hanging heavy in the air like leaded fog dissipates. When the timer on my phone goes off at three minutes, one might assume that someone in the room would shout and break the uncomfortable silence like they'd been holding their breath the whole time, but they don't. I never rush our entrance back into dialogue; rather, I wait and allow students to speak first. What's crazy is that, generally speaking, most students go nearly another minute or so before saying anything.

I use this excruciatingly painful exercise to bring awareness to the concept of impatient space and the latent tension lurking in the shadows of each passing moment. If our attention spans are not "fed" regularly, the withdrawal symptoms kick in almost immediately, as though we were one of Pavlov's pooches or Skinner's manipulated rodents.

A study at the University of Virginia with over 700 participants placed people alone in a room, where they were asked to sit and do nothing for anywhere from 6 to 15 minutes. They were given a button and told they could press the button like a "safe word," but if they did press it, then it would deliver a painful electric shock. Let me reiterate: SIX to FIFTEEN fucking minutes of being alone, which is about 2-5 typical rock songs, a couple of YouTube videos, or the time it takes to make and eat a bowl of cereal. Still, 67% of the men in the study and 25% of the women pressed the fucking button, thereby choosing to experience searing physical pain rather than sit and do nothing, which is literally the simplest thing in the world any of us can do while conscious.

This study is far from unique, as an increasing number of studies show that the majority of today's humans would rather experience pain than boredom, to which I respond: what the fuck? Maybe it's because I'm a complete and inconsolable wuss when it comes to pain (except for tattoos, of course – those are addictive and really rad), or perhaps it's because I'm fully aware of the benefits of boredom, which I'll discuss momentarily, but I simply cannot fucking begin to fathom how someone might prefer physical pain to a wee bit of mental discomfort.

What is this terrifying concept of boredom such that so many of us would as soon harm ourselves rather than experience? Scientists at York University defined boredom as the unpleasant experience of wanting to engage in satisfying activity but being unable to fulfill that craving, which suggests that, when we experience boredom, we are disengaging from internal thoughts and feelings (whether by choice or unintentionally) while simultaneously failing to find interest in external happenings. Basically, being bored means that the shit around us is wholly uninteresting, while our heads are full of shit we'd rather not think about. The same scientists, however, stated that most of us attribute our boredom to our environment, completely ignoring the fact that we're avoiding our thoughts like they were that one dude from high school who dropped out of college to become an insurance agent and now tries to contact everyone he went to school through LinkedIn to talk about term life insurance.

Okay, we know what boredom is (as if we really needed a scientific definition, but hey, now you can impress your friends or win big on Jeopardy someday), but what causes it, or more importantly, what makes it appear so unattractive that most of us avoid it in favor of pain? Let's check in with American psychologist, Robert Plutchik. This dude named, defined, and categorized primary human emotions, starting with the eight most basic — trust, fear, surprise, sadness, disgust, anger, anticipation, and joy — followed by eight lesser variants of those basic emotions — acceptance, apprehension, distraction, pensiveness, *boredom*, annoyance, interest, and serenity. Pursuant to his research, boredom is apparently a subset of disgust. Essentially, disgust is a survival emotion that helps us avoid pretty shitty stuff, such as, well, shit. When we open up an old takeout box of General Tso's chicken and see that it's growing hair, we don't think, "I'm so proud of you, little chicken pieces! You've finally hit puberty!" No, instead, we think, "Goddamn, I need to clean the fridge. That's nasty." Then, we either throw it away so it doesn't infect the rest of our food, or we put it back and hope someone else in the house deals with it. Disgust, in a sense, keeps us alive, while boredom, on the other hand, doesn't – or does it? When we get bored, it's the brain's way of notifying us that we're no longer engaged, and it's time to move on. That's where the problems start.

Remember earlier when we talked about the 'attention economy' and how all these entities vying for our attention all day, every day, are slowly turning us into lower-order animals who have little to no control over where we direct our attention? When that boredom kicks in, we automatically start hunting for something engaging; it's natural instinct, at least, for most of us. When we have convenient little electronic devices waiting in our pockets that happen to be connected to zettabytes of information (some useful, some not) at the flick of a finger, our brains impulsively reach for them. You may be thinking, "Gosh, that doesn't make it sound so bad!" In an ideal world, no, it's not *totally* bad. If I pick my phone up and look up Einstein's theory of special relativity or read a long-form think piece about the role of Plutchik's emotion wheel in diagnosing mental illness, then I'm utilizing that little device in a positively reinforcing manner to learn and expand my knowledge base.

But that's not what we do with our phones, is it?

We have Candy Crush.

We have social media.

We have Snapchat filters.

We have Flappy Bird (or at least, we did at one point).

If we think of digital information as food, where the aforementioned article on the emotion wheel represents something hearty or good for us like lasagna or steamed broccoli, then apps like Candy Crush are the equivalent of sweet, sticky, fatty dessert. We're basically skipping what we know is good for us and going straight for the sweets.

Boredom, then, is like a psychological safety switch. Whereas disgust protects us from encounters with microbiological baddies, its subtler form, boredom, can be a sign that either: A) we're overstimulated and need some time away from all those notifications shouting LOOK AT ME all day long;

or, B) we're not challenged enough, and it's time for some variety and diversity to re-engage our brains in a positive manner. Speaking of which, new research into boredom concludes that boredom actually lowers brain activity by up to 5%, and as a result, that deficiency significantly sparks creativity.

Researchers at the University of Central Lancashire performed a fascinating experiment with participants who were directed to copy numbers out of a phone book for an extended period (sounds so fucking fun, right?), and if they survived this menial task, then they were asked to take a test that measured creative thinking, such as devising as many uses for a pair of cups as possible. The bored test subjects FAR outscored their more entertained counterparts in a control group. Dr. Sandi Mann, the researcher behind this torture test, concluded that boredom can ignite creativity by forcing us to wrestle with the problem of emptiness when it comes to these slower moments. Furthermore, she expressed concern for the modern condition by concluding, "We try to extinguish every moment of boredom in our lives with mobile devices," which temporarily puts a stop to the discomfort of boredom but also eliminates the possibility of deeper thinking when it comes to such grappling with what to do or what to think. Playing with our phones as opposed to confronting boredom as it occurs, she noted, "is like eating junk food."

It has long been understood by neuroscience that placing limits on ourselves sparks creativity. We don't need research to remind us of this; all it takes is a little exercise in imagination. If an artist is given a canvas the size of an acre and told to paint what-the-fuck-ever comes to mind, then the artist will struggle with where to begin and how to fill all that space. However, give that same artist a blank postcard and say the end result should be an existential reflection of the current state of humankind as a result of the lack of connectivity brought on by life in the Age of Distraction, and the artist will be in the zone in no time flat. As limitations are imposed, our brains use the challenges posed by those limits to fill in those gaps with new connections through the process of *bricolage*, or the construction of novel solutions using previously unrelated and/or dissimilar materials.

Creativity has been measured regularly in several longitudinal studies, including one at the College of William & Mary, where researchers found that kids' creativity scores steadily increased each year until 1990, at which point, they started declining. Scientists initially said that one little hiccup in the trend wasn't enough to grow alarmed, but then, as they watched, the numbers continued dropping and are still falling today. At first, they pointed fingers at the usual suspects: television, video games, lack of creativity development in schools, abhorrent teacher pay, standardized testing, etc. However, current research suggests that this perhaps may be connected to a general lack of downtime—boredom—in which that deeper thinking can take place.

Look, I can spout off all the research in the world, but it's highly unlikely all this scholarly, academic, book-smart bullshit is going to transform any of us into cheerleaders for boredom. Boredom fucking sucks. It's uncomfortable. But if you haven't grown more intrigued after reading about all the science surrounding boredom, then reflect on the following quote from a student of mine who took part in the exercise I will propose that you try at the conclusion of this chapter: "If I can't bring myself to be comfortable with my own thoughts, then how in the hell can I expect anyone else to want to be alone with me?"

Damn.

One more time, a little louder for the people in the cheap seats:

"If I can't bring myself to be comfortable with my own thoughts, then how in the hell can I expect anyone else to want to be alone with me?"

Maybe the thought of being alone as a means of sparking creativity doesn't do the trick. Perhaps the idea of encouraging deeper and more meaningful thought doesn't inspire you to pursue alone time. If none of that works and sparks your interest in the idea of dropping the fucking phone in favor of doing literally nothing, then perhaps knowing that spending regular time alone (and bored!) is a step toward greater self-awareness, which develops empathy, compassion, understanding, and promotes connection with others. Being alone and bored allows us to process, dissect, and analyze the thoughts that we've been shoving to the side rather than confronting.

I'd be willing to bet that many, if not most of us, are, at best, hesitant to, and at worst, afraid to face the thoughts or feelings that may arise when all the noise dissipates and we're left standing alone with whatever bullshit bubbles up. In fact, the more we procrastinate and keep ourselves busy as a means of avoiding such a confrontation, the more likely there really *is* some serious shit hiding, something unpleasant we've pushed down into the dark corners of our minds, hoping it never surfaces again. Being alone with our thoughts requires courage; it requires us to face those thoughts and feelings, accept them for what they are, and allow them to pass after examining them carefully. If those same thoughts and feelings continue resurfacing every time we're alone, then that's a pretty damn good sign that maybe we need some help dealing with those once and for all. This idea of something resurfacing again and again is better known as *ruminating*, where our minds spin like a goddamn hamster wheel that never stops turning. I'm sure a lot of us reading this book (myself included) have a bad habit of lying awake at night, revisiting the day or worrying about the next. Why?

It's a lot like when there's a piece of popcorn stuck in your teeth. You know it's there, but what do we do every five seconds that pass and it's still not fucking gone? We tongue the shit out of it, hitting it from every conceivable angle, using different techniques and pressures, pining for a piece of fucking floss. Those thoughts that keep circling are a lot like that. Maybe someone said something that really dug in under our skin, and of course, we think of the ultimate comeback about 30 minutes after the situation is over and the person is gone. We take that conversation to the shower, where we win the argument no less than 90 fucking times before the hot water runs out. If this sounds familiar, listen up.

What do we do for a song that's stuck on repeat? Do we listen to the song over and over again, hoping maybe a different song will play, even though the screen clearly displays "Repeat[1]" as the option highlighted? Nope. We change the repeat option so we can move to a new song. Being alone with these thoughts and learning to take them off repeat is no easy task, but the trick lies in noticing the thought, acknowledging what it is and where it comes from, and then finally allowing the thought to continue on its merry fucking way without latching onto it. Think of the mind as a snow globe, where, as we get agitated, each thought is a piece of glitter. What do we do with a snow globe? We watch as each of the glitter flakes flitter and flicker their way back to the bottom. For some people, the act of doing so brings a smile to their faces, so why shouldn't the rest of us do the same thing with our thoughts?

A particularly helpful analogy used by the Zen master, Thich Nhat Hanh, is that of a cloudy sky. If a clear, blue sky represents perfect contentment and happiness, and clouds represent thoughts that won't get the fuck out of the way, then it makes sense that sometimes, the sky is pretty clear, while other times, it's overcast and dreary. At those times, despair sets in, and it might feel pretty hopeless. Seeing as how most of us tend to focus on what's immediately in front of us, it makes sense that we might assume that the clouds are all there is, but what if we could move the clouds? Essentially, that's what taking time out of our day to do nothing accomplishes. As we acknowledge each cloud and allow it to pass by without latching on to it, they lose the power to occupy our minds in an ongoing basis without paying rent. Before we know it, there's at least a bit of blue showing through, and that, my friends, represents hope. With that hope, we can continue building upon that success as a means of acknowledging and releasing ourselves from some of the bigger clouds blocking our exposure to that coveted UV light.

But none of that is going to happen until we learn to put the fucking phone down and spend some time alone.

### Chapter Challenge: One is the Awesomest Number

As soon as possible and before moving on to the next chapter, set aside one hour to be alone. Yes, one full hour alone, and during that hour, spend your time in honest, thoughtful reflection. You should not bring along your phone, books, electronics, music, pets, other people, small children, etc. Spend this hour completely and totally alone. A lot of people find it helpful to go on a hike or walk in nature somewhere, thereby removing the temptation to say "screw this" and watch Netflix instead. During the first 15 minutes or so of the hour, as a thought arises, practice noticing the thought, acknowledging its existence, and allowing it to pass.

Then, spend the rest of the hour reflecting on your most important relationships. Perhaps take the temperature of these relationships in a general sense at first and then examine each one individually, working your way from most important to those of lesser significance. Think about what's good and strong in those relationships, but also consider that which could use improvement. Use this time to develop self-awareness of areas in your life that you would like to improve, and be specific. Saying to yourself, "I want to be a nicer person" is a good start, but it doesn't give you a lot to work with later. As we progress through this book, the various areas for improvement that you think of here are going to come into play again later, so the more specific your chosen issue or situation, the better this book will be for those relationships.

Once the hour is up, jot down notes on your hour alone. List off all the issues or situations you'd like to work on later, but don't worry about addressing them yet. Simply identify those areas for improvement that you think might have a big impact on your most significant relationships.

# PART II:

## PUT THE FUCKING PHONE DOWN & STOP USING IT AS A CRUTCH

In the second part of our journey through this profanity-enriched discourse in mindful presence, we'll examine how life might look different if we simply push the boundaries of our comfort zones. For some of us, the time we spend sitting within the walls of those comfort zones allows such boundaries to solidify, so pushing against them could prove more difficult for some than others, whose comfort zone boundaries are more the consistency of cherry-flavored gelatin. Part of un-fucking ourselves out from within a self-induced rut involves a process with a delightfully wicked name: perturbation. No, this isn't self-love. Get your mind out of the gutter. To perturb something is to cause anxiety or make things feel a bit uneasy. You may ask yourself, why in the blistering fuck would I willingly make myself feel uneasy? We do it all the time: rollercoasters, skydiving, karaoke, asking someone out or expressing love to someone for the first time. We willingly perturb ourselves without second thoughts; however, when perturbation involves more conscious or obvious discomfort, we often tend to avoid it.

This part of the book is comprised of four chapters, each of which methodically and carefully pushes back against the resistance of conformity and consistency — our comfort zones. We'll learn to find out what others *really* think of us and how to cope with that, how wonderful it feels to defy social judgment, how to enjoy being wrong, and what's so fucking incredible about vulnerability. Hmm, when I put it all that way, maybe it doesn't sound all that fun, but trust me. Have I let you down so far? Don't answer that.

For us to change, it has to start with more than desire. Anyone can want to learn to swim, but until we drop into the frigid chill of the water for the first time, all that desire is pure bullshit. Think of this section of the book as dipping your toes in the water. Learning to swim simply prepares us for what comes later.

# 4

# ENLIGHTENMENT ISN'T ALL KITTENS & UNICORNS

Late on a somewhat chilly Friday autumn evening, I took a break from an intense session of first-person shooter games to go have a smoke on the steps to my single-wide trailer in northern Idaho. Behind me, as I walked out the door, trailed a good friend who was visiting from Washington State University in Pullman, about 100 miles or so away. My friend made the long drive up to where my wife and I had recently moved to be closer to family, and it was the first time I'd seen him since resigning from the physics lab where we met and worked together. Drinking our cheap, watered-down beer (I was probably on my fourth or eighth beer by that moment), we sucked away on our cancer delivery tubes and reminisced about old times while my wife rolled her eyes lovingly in the background.

By the way, not that it's any of your business, but I quit smoking in 2006, and I haven't smoked since. What a shitty habit. If you smoke, do yourself a favor and quit. I know, such unique advice, but seriously – don't wait to quit. Do it now.

Anyway, as we shaved minutes off our lives with each successive puff, I started musing on what a great moment it was, only to be interrupted by my friend, who said, "Goddammit, Josh, I fucking hate it when you do that."

Dumbfounded, shocked, and maybe adding a dash of melodrama, I looked back at my friend, bewildered. "Huh? What did I do?"

"Don't play stupid, Josh," he condescended, "You checked out of the conversation, and now, you're thinking of what you want to say next, probably something to one-up me."

I gasped, probably sounding like a southern scoundrel, clutching my pearls at the thought of my honor being tarnished so heartlessly and deliberately. "I most certainly did NOT! I have no idea wha . . ."

"Yes, you did," he cut me off, "You do it all the time, man. Drives me fucking crazy. Always has."

"But . . ." I interjected as I looked to my wife for moral support, and that's when I saw her nodding in agreement. I gasped again, cranking up my self-righteous indignation all the way to eleven.

"Oh yeah?" I questioned, channeling my inner toddler, "If I do it all the time, then tell me this, smart guy, why is this the first time I'm hearing about it?" Yes, I thought, the perfect comeback. I had him on the defensive, and there was no coming back from that. At least, that's how it sounded in my head.

"Ha!" my friend laughed, taking another puff from his coffin nail, "It's because you turn into a raging asshole any time someone criticizes you!"

Ouch. That hurt. I felt my defenses rising up to meet him, sort of like Storm from the X-Men, as her eyes turn white when she summons the power of the elements to smite her enemies. My friend was practically begging to be smitten, and it was my responsibility to give it to him, but just as I was about to go all crazy-superhero on my friend, a gut instinct stopped me. I turned to my wife, half-expecting what I knew I would see, and sure enough, there she was, still nodding in agreement. "Yep . . ." she added, "he's not wrong."

Somehow, at that moment, it felt like the fall sky opened up and shone the light of the heavens down on me, illuminating me as I wondered if this was really how I'd acted toward every person in my life. Regardless, I put my proverbial tail between my legs and apologized for my momentary lapse of attention, and it felt really fucking liberating to come clean. In the back of my mind, I vowed to look into it further when I was sober.

The next day, I called up someone who had known me for more than a decade by that time, and I asked him if he had time for a question. When he agreed, I asked if he'd ever noticed me checking out of a conversation and appearing to be thinking of the next thing I wanted to say. He took all of 16 milliseconds to respond: "Holy shit, yes! You do it all the fucking time! Drives me up the fucking wall, man!"

Shit.

"Fair enough," I continued, "but why haven't you told me sooner?" I flinched in preparation for his response.

"Jesus fucking Christ, Josh, I have! Are you really this dense? Literally every time I call you out on it, you turn into a raging asshole like you do any other time someone criticizes you!"

Double down on the shit, please, and let it ride.

My dad used to have a saying he loved tossing around as I was growing up: If everyone calls you a horse, then at least check for a tail. In less than 12 hours, I had three people, all who knew me pretty goddamn well, tell me the same fucking thing. These people had the most invested in our relationships, so they had no reason to sugar-coat it or walk on eggshells with me.

Simply put, I was straight shook. I began wondering how many others perceived me the same way but were either too afraid to tell me or tried to tell me, and I failed to listen. How many of my relationships failed because of my inability to listen and take constructive criticism? I pulled out a notebook and started writing down every last friend or romantic relationship that ended abruptly, along with friends whom I no longer spoke to. Next to each one, I tried to articulate the original reasons why I thought the relationship had failed. Once I finished my melancholic list, I replaced my reasoning with the potential for no listening and being a defensive prick, and in more than 90% of the cases, the newfound reason made more sense that what I once believed.

What happened was a revelation of my *blind spot.* We all act differently around different people and in diverse situations, and we can think of these various 'selves' as being one of four panes of a window:

- The *public self* is the one everyone knows. We know it and others know it; this is the unhidden part of ourselves.
- The *private self* is that side of me I reserve for only me. This is comprised of information about me that I choose to keep from everyone else, and I am clearly aware of it.
- The *unknown self* is easy; this is information nobody knows about me; not others and not even myself.
- The fourth type, *the blind spot*, is the most dangerous by a long shot. The blind spot is comprised of information everyone else knows about me, yet, I remain oblivious.

Sometimes, blind spot information could be positive, such as a person who is super generous but perhaps doesn't realize it. Explaining to that person that she or he is generous might result in some humble attempts to deflect the praise, but it won't likely result in conflict. Shit like that is rare, though.

The blind spot typically builds up from pieces of our more negative qualities because, quite frankly, most of us aren't in a hurry to learn about the things we do to piss others off. As a result, we stuff that shit down into the shadows of our minds where it calcifies, we ignore it, and then it comes back to bite us in the fucking ass when we least expect it. However, by acknowledging these qualities in ourselves and confronting how they impact the people around us, we develop an ability to take control over how we present ourselves to others.

You may hear some people drop some motivational poster sounding bullshit like, "I don't let what others think of me affect the way I see myself."

Horseshit. Completely unfiltered, emerging straight from the equine cornhole, unrefined, still-steaming horse excrement.

Each and every one of us have incredibly complex identities that are forged in the fires of our daily interactions throughout our lives. The way we see ourselves is affected by the way others see us and how they articulate those perceptions back to us. If someone tells a child she's worthless, she'll grow up believing she's worthless—not because she actually is—but because we tend to internalize the perceptions of others into our own self-perceptions. This is called the *looking glass self* and has deep roots in scientific research, so the next time someone tries bragging about being wholly unaffected by others' opinions, remember that it's not your responsibility to enlighten them; maybe they need a friend, some cheap beer, and a smoke to find out for themselves. Actually, disregard the smoke. Stick to brewdogs and good conversation. For us to lessen the impact of the blind spot, we need to actively seek feedback from others on how they see us, in an attempt to unite how we see ourselves with others' perceptions as well.

None of that will happen until we learn to put the fucking phone down and start finding out how others really see us.

### Chapter Challenge: Checking the Blind Spot

It is extremely likely that this chapter's challenge is the most difficult one of the entire book, so it's pretty cool that we're knocking it out early on. You'll thank me later. Approach this activity with courage and trust that, once you've finished, you'll find that it is also likely to be the most valuable and rewarding activity in the long run.

To check your blind spot, choose someone you care about: a close friend, a family member, a good mentor, or a loved one. Pick someone you trust and with whom you want to improve your relationship, and invite that person to share a good meal. It's up to you whether you go out for the meal or make it at home, but regardless, this should be delectable food that takes more time to eat and naturally causes you to eat slowly, deliberately, enjoying every last morsel.

Great conversations happen over great food, and you'll notice that I propose this relatively often during other activities dispersed throughout the book. Relatively few activities in regular human life involve inserting things into our bodies; eating food is one of those activities, while the others are a topic for a different book that I'm not prepared to author quite yet. Think about it: when we eat, we're entrusting the person who prepared our food to not have poisoned it or done anything malicious to it. We pop it in our mouths without thinking too much about it, unless, of course, we're doing the mindful eating exercise. That act of trust goes a long way toward creating and sustaining meaningful moments, so good food it is for this exercise.

As you share this meal together, tell the person that you have a question to ask, but before popping the question, explain the ground rules. You are not allowed to respond defensively or rebut in any way. The only responses you're allowed are clarifying questions that keep the conversation moving. Assure the other person that there will be absolutely no negative consequences, whether short-term or longer-term, as a result of their responses to the question you're about to ask. Your job as they answer is to strictly listen mindfully and with an open heart and mind.

Once you've set the ground rules, pop the question: "What is the one thing about me that bugs you the most?"

As you can guess, this is a fucking tough activity, and there's going to be a butt-load of anxiety that goes along with it. Presuming you've asked someone whose opinion matters to you, as the directions explicitly stated, then this person means a lot to you, and why is that? It's because of the looking glass self. This person's opinion of you is intricately tied to how you see yourself, so potentially damaging information coming from that person is likely to impact your self-image. Also, there's always the slight chance that the other person launches a ballistic truth missile that, once it hits, you can never un-hear. Not being able to defend yourself gives that person permission to unload things they may not have offered up otherwise, and as a result, we're likely to listen much more deeply. Remember the chapter on listening? This is your chance to practice mindful listening, so it may be helpful to go back and re-read it before this meal.

I'm not going to sit here and write this book like some fucking hypocrite, either, so don't think I haven't done this myself. Granted, I told you the story of the first time, which wasn't even over a good meal; all we had was burning tobacco and cheap, shitty beer. I've been employing this exercise in my interpersonal communication classes since 2012, and I always do the activity alongside my students, to show them that I'm willing to either put up or shut the fuck up. This means that I've done this activity at least 15 times as of this writing, and I'll likely keep doing it at least a few times a year, because it gets better every time I do it. In all the years I've done it, I have yet to experience a negative result. Furthermore, I have yet for a student to report anything but a profound experience as a result of taking part. Regardless of the fear and anxiety leading up to it and the discomfort we feel as our comfort zone boundaries are being redrawn, this exercise presents the key to a door that opens into a whole new understanding of ourselves and how others see us.

However, not only is the content of the other person's response valuable, but so is the way in which they answer. For example, if they rebut instantly off the top of their heads, or worse, if they say something like, "Excellent, I've been waiting for this day," as they reach for their wallet and pull out a well-worn list, then this tells you that maybe you've been a bit of a dick. On the other hand, if the person takes a while to respond, maybe that means things are going pretty well. Or, it could mean the person is still afraid of the consequences of being honest. Maybe a bit of prodding and encouragement could help in such a situation.

Ultimately, the core of this exercise is rooted in a word that we'll come back to several times in this book, and that is the dreaded v-word: *vulnerability*. We'll cover this concept in more depth in a future chapter, but for now, understand that to be vulnerable is to open ourselves up to potential attack, willingly, for the purpose of stretching that comfort zone, and becoming stronger people all around.

One of the most mind-blowingly vulnerable times I ever did this exercise was relatively recent. In all the times I've done it, I've almost always asked the question of a family member such as my wife or children, because they matter more to me than any other human. But for the instance in question, I chose a coworker I've known for more than a decade. Why I didn't ask her sooner, I don't know. That's a lie. Actually, I do know. It's because I was fucking scared.

Before I went to her office to ask the dreaded question, my palms were sweating, knees weak, arms were heavy. There was vomit on my sweater already, and I think it was pasta I had at my mom's the night before. I lost myself in the moment for sure, but all Eminem references aside, I seriously felt like I was ready to shit myself. I think the reason why was related to that comfort zone boundary. In all the years of doing this activity, I had grown comfortable with my family's responses. They were familiar and predictable. But at work, I'm a different person. What if my peer told me I was being an arrogant prick who never listens? What if the old Josh resurfaced, and I hadn't noticed it? What if there's some totally new issue like "mansplaining" or something worse that I wasn't aware of? In other words, what if how I saw myself before asking her the question was horrifyingly wrong, and as I walked out of her office, I learned that I was the same little boy from before who fucked up every relationship of his young life?

Fortunately for my fragile male ego, her response was alarmingly tame. She told me that I have a tendency to take on too much work at once and, as a result, she worries about me burning out too soon. Of course, I responded, "Are you sure that's it?" I had a hard time believing it was, but she assured me that she was being bluntly honest with me, at which point, she began praising all my other great qualities, which I've taken the liberty of typing up and framing in my office for everyone to see how awesome I am, according to my coworker. Yes, of course, I'm kidding. I'm not that conceited. I had it laminated.

Every time I conduct this exercise, I slowly chip away at the ego that got in the way of all my past relationships. With each uncomfortable interaction like this, I expand my comfort zone, increase self-awareness, reinforce relationships, and increase my resilience to confronting criticism, thereby using it as a tool rather than perceiving it as an attack. Not once have I left this exercise thinking it was awful, and I never want to do it again. Every fucking time, I have concluded my reflections on the exercise with, "I can't wait to do this again," and my students each semester tell me the same.

Now, it's your turn. As you seek out criticism from someone you care about, pay attention to how it feels to hear it. If that ever-familiar heat of defensiveness starts warming up your ears, simply notice it, acknowledge it, and allow it to pass, just like those thoughts at the end of the last chapter when you spent time alone. Notice how it feels to let those urges pass unheeded, and continue listening and empathizing instead. Once the interaction is done, and the two of you part ways, take some time to write down in clear detail what the other person said about you. Write it down (yes, like good old handwriting), as much as you might not want to write it down. As you recount the person's responses, perhaps add to them by speculating on where your behaviors might come from. Maybe imagine how it might feel if someone did that same behavior to you. Once you've effectively written all this down, do the following to finish off this activity.

Take that piece of paper and destroy it, but get creative and make sure that paper goes out in style. Here's some ideas I've found particularly satisfying:

- Burn it (but use lots of lighter fluid so the flames are really big, you crazy pyromaniac) *
- Run over it with your car (or if possible, roast your tires on top of it) *
- Use it for target practice *
- Black out the page with a permanent marker or black spray paint (and then burn it) *
- Make confetti out of the page with a chainsaw *
- Dissolve it in acid, a la Walter White *

Regardless of the method you choose, as you destroy it, focus on how it feels to symbolically release yourself from this behavior. Make a mental commitment to reduce or eliminate the behavior in the spirit of promoting and nurturing healthier, more positive relationships. Let go, and allow yourself to be reborn.

* Please do not:

- Burn down your home, anyone else's home or property, or yourself;
- Get into an accident;
- Shoot at or near anything that shouldn't be shot;
- Make yourself pass out from sniffing fumes;

- Make hamburger out of a much-needed limb;
- Accidentally dissolve yourself, either partially or in full;
- Place yourself or anyone else in harm's way.

Any of these outcomes will most certainly prevent you from being able to continue with the book. Plus, that would really suck, so please use your best judgment. If you don't have judgment, borrow someone else's for the time being.

# 5

# FUCK SOCIAL JUDGMENT

Let's start this chapter with another lovely imagination exercise: If you could do anything you wanted in public without fear of judgment, guilt, shame, or criticism, what would it be? Okay, let me add *legally* to the question, in case that changes things. What would it be? Would you sing your favorite hair metal ballad in a sober karaoke session? Perhaps you might take your significant other out dancing. Maybe you'd stand up in front of a crowd of important, highly influential people, and pour your heart out by sharing a message for which your passion glows hot. You might even leave the house with zero fucks to give, no makeup on, and hair in a side pony. Hell, if you're a dude, maybe that means finally rocking the man-bun.

Think about what all these possibilities represent. These, along with whatever you thought of when first reading the question, are enjoyable life experiences that allow you to express yourself as an individual, but they're also things we aren't doing, and why not? The answer lies in our utter fear of social judgment. We'll explore that in a moment, but first, a story.

I was on my way home after picking up my kids from school. As we turned a busy corner, we saw a man holding a prominent cardboard sign, and on the sign, were two simple words with a profound message: YOU MATTER. This grabbed our attention, and we watched as we waited for the light to change. This man stood there, moving around, singing loudly, and pointing at people as they drove by, waving his sign at them and shouting an accompanying reminder that, yes, we all matter. People honked, waved, and smiled. Several people pulled into the gas station parking lot, got out of their cars, and ran over to him before giving him a big hug. As we watched the scene unfold, I thought about how it must have felt for him.

The amount of personal satisfaction must have been absolutely off the fucking chart for that guy. Then, I wondered if I could do it, and if I'm being honest, I don't think I could. It's not because I don't want to, nor is it because I don't believe in the concept. The real reason? Because I'm scared that people would think I'm: homeless, begging for money, insincere, stupid, or some fruity-ass liberal hippie on drugs. Here's the crazy bit: Did I think the guy on the corner was ANY of those things? Fuck no. I admired the shit out of him and silently wished I could be more like him. That realization was profound.

Back to the question from the start of the chapter: Let's look at my examples, along with a typical response from most of us:

- "I'd love to sing Journey's *Anyway You Want It* in a crowded bar, but . . ."
- "Sure, it would be great to go out dancing, but . . ."
- "It would be a dream come true to inspire others, but . . ."
- "Hell yes, I'd look great with a man-bun, but . . ."

Notice what each one of these responses has in common, other than their striking ability to relate with most of us? One word: BUT. How often do we use that specific conjunction to deny ourselves the activities we love?

- "Makeup takes so goddamn long to put on, *but* I don't want anyone to see me without it."
- "Sweats/pajamas/yoga pants are so comfy, *but* I'd hate to run into someone I know while I look like that."
- "I'd so love to ask out that girl or guy, *but* I know they're going to say no."
- "The beach is so much fun, *but* nobody wants to see this dad-bod shirtless."

How many of these phrases have we all used before, or how many similar phrases have we caught ourselves saying? Maybe it's time to break these phrases down and look at them closer:

1. First, there's an acknowledgment of the potential joy or pleasure that comes as a result of the activity;
2. Second, there's the BUT, which alerts us to the prevalence of fear or anxiety preventing us from taking part in said activity;
3. And third, there's that all-too-familiar assumption that others will judge us for having a bit of fucking fun in our lives, and often, that might also come with a half-cocked invention of an excuse as to why we can't take part.

As a result, we stay home and play games on our phones. We sit on the sidelines, faces buried in fucking screens. We consciously and intentionally allow others' opinions of us to dictate the amount of joy we allow into our lives, and the worst part is that others probably don't even have those opinions. We only *assume* that's what they think. Then, we lie to ourselves about why we chose not to participate in said activities because we assume that admitting this fear makes us appear weak, but acknowledging that fear is the first step toward remediating it. Nobody, I repeat, nobody is immune to these fears. Even the most confident among us still have a tendency to hold back with certain activities because of a latent fear of social judgment, and that fear is precisely what we're here to address in this chapter.

**What We Expect vs. What Actually Happens**

It never fails. I've been teaching public speaking classes since 2008, and within each and every one, there are two types of students. Type 1 is cocky and thinks he or she (if I'm being honest, it's a 'he' 90% of the time) can wing it and get by on personality and confidence alone. Type 2 is uncertain, anxious, and wavering in every aspect of confidence. Guess which type gives better speeches?

If you're reading this, and you're Type 1, then I'm sorry to have to make a truth strafing run, but Type 2 wins. Every. Damn. Time. The overconfident person will get up and try to make everyone laugh. He'll meander around his topic, completely disorganized, but he'll do so with style and with few fillers (um, uh, you know, like, etc.). In other words, he's all show and abso-fucking-lutely no depth.

Type 2 usually gets up to speak after Type 1 (Type 1 always volunteers to go first, probably as a side effect of overconfidence), and you can easily see Type 2's confidence shaken a bit, thinking they have to live up to Type 1's clown show. Nervously and cautiously, Type 2 opens up a bit at a time, blundering through a few meager fillers and trying to make their way. Of course, by their second or third speech, Type 2 has won over everyone in the room and delivered the most phenomenal, touching/moving, well-researched, and carefully structured speeches of the entire class. Type 1, interestingly enough, usually drops out of the class by that point, once they realize the strategy of 'winging it' doesn't work. Eventually, Type 1 returns to my classroom and retakes the class, years later, as a born-again Type 2.

Types 1 and 2 have vastly different expectations. Type 1 heads into his speech with the expectation that charm, a few stupid jokes, and a rebellious, self-destructive attitude toward school is enough to get by, while Type 2 heads into her speech with healthy fear, and it is precisely that healthy fear that causes Type 2 to actually fucking prepare her speech in advance. Motivated by a fear of embarrassment, failure, or even a fear of boring the audience, Type 2 writes and researches the piss out of her speech early (following my advice instead of ignoring it). She learns about her audience and looks for methods to connect with them during her speech. She also practices the shit out of her speech so she knows exactly what to expect when game day rolls around. In a nutshell, Type 1 operates from a set of confidence-inspired delusions, while Type 2 has perceptions that are grounded in reality. Instead of ignoring her fear, she embraces and acknowledges that fear, using it to make herself better.

This chapter's challenge (at the end of the chapter) asks us to tap into those perceptions and examine them to determine if they're more based in delusion or reality, and if I'm being blunt here, odds are, they're somewhat delusional. Don't close the book and call me an asshole just yet; stick around and read my own delusional horror stories.

## The Green Card

While in between my first and second marriage, I spent a lot of time in bars with my friends. One of our favorite haunts was a delightfully quaint Irish pub in downtown Spokane that made the best Guinness-battered fish and chips. One evening, I noticed all the signed dollar bills stapled to the walls, so I asked the bartender what they meant. "Earn your green card, and you can put a dollar on the wall," he responded.

Okay, I'll bite. "What the green card?"

"Sing an Irish drinking song, and you get a green card, which gets you 20% off your first drink for life and priority seating on St. Patrick's Day."

Did he just say we had to sing? To the whole fucking bar? Fuck. That. Shit. Not a chance. My resistance lasted at least two more beers before my friend and I started talking about when we were going to earn our green cards. We went home that night and hit the YouTube machine, looking for a good Irish drinking song since neither of us knew any. Like a good nerd, I typed up the lyrics and printed them out for reference. God, I'm an embarrassment. We spent time over the next week practicing to make sure we could pull it off, and we decided on the following Friday for our bar concert.

Of course, being a Friday, the pub was much busier than any other night, but that didn't matter. After a few Newcastle Brown Ales, we were nearly ready, so we approached the bartender and told him we wanted our green cards, ready to sing for him. At that moment, he looked just a wee bit too excited at the proposition, which was the first of many unanticipated red flags.

"All right," he affirmed us as he patted the bar top, "up on the bar."

"Wait, what the fuck?" I asked. "Did you just fucking say ON the fucking bar?" If you think I curse a lot typing out this book, you should see me inebriated.

"Yep. To get the green card, you have to stand on the bar and sing an Irish drinking song."

Um, nobody fucking told us that, but we were committed at this point. The bartender reached under the bar, turned off the music, and retrieved a really big fucking brass bell, which he rang out several times, announcing to the entire bloody world that these "two fine, young men" were going to sing us all a song.

It was like I had an out-of-body experience. Sheer will and a fear of looking even stupider for having backed down launched my ass on top of that bar, and some unknown, untapped confidence reached into my jacket pocket for the folded-up song lyrics. We belted out "The Pub with No Beer" horribly off-key, and neither rhythm nor self-respect was anywhere to be found. I was convinced that, if I wasn't on some hidden camera show, the crowd was going to get ugly once we were done and start throwing bottles and various fruits and vegetables at us. We were truly awful, a drunken sight to behold. Two minutes later, however, as we hit the grand finale, the crowd fully erupted into cheers and applause. The scenario I imagined never materialized; in fact, it turned out to be the exact opposite. We stapled our dollars to the wall that night and joined the O'Doherty's family, despite my lack of Irish ancestry.

Following that evening, I discovered a new sense of confidence. After all, if I could sing on top of a bar (without backup or accompaniment of any kind) in front of total strangers and somehow make it an entertaining spectacle, then what the actual fuck was stopping me from anything else? It was also one of the first times in my life when I realized that expectations and reality don't mix well together. And, good lord almighty, I am so glad there were no phones around back then to record us and post it to social media.

### Whoops

Confession: I was never a traditional college student. After I graduated high school and in accordance with the arrogant asshole I was (see my blind spot story in the previous chapter), I told my father I didn't want to go to college. My brilliant reasoning? I was already smart enough, and I didn't need no goddamn piece of paper to prove it. What a supreme dick, right? I went into the workforce and eventually landed myself a blue-collar manufacturing job, where I spent a total of eight years of my life while working my way up the ladder into a lucrative engineering position. Not bad for a 20-something with no degree, I have to admit, but don't congratulate me, because the company I worked for was bought out by a global conglomerate that had a strict policy of not promoting people without degrees, placing me smack-dab in the middle of a seemingly impossible decision.

Fuck. Now what?

At 28, I found myself facing the prospect of either sticking around for another 40 years of doing the same exact job without advancement or leaving and heading off to college. This revelation took place mere weeks before getting married to the best fucking woman I've ever known, and thanks to her support and myopic, misguided belief in me, college was exactly where we ended up. More specifically, we moved to Pullman, Washington, where I began studying physics and computer science at Washington State University, and this is where I met my friend, the one who so kindly showed me what an asshole I was.

Anyone who has ever been to Pullman knows that it's basically a miniature version of San Francisco (i.e., an ass-load of steep-as-all-balls hills with stairs for a sidewalk), but with piles of snow for six months out of the year. And when I state 'miniature,' I mean there's a population of about 30,000 or so during the school year, and 25,000 of those people are the student body. The rest of the year, it's a farming community.

I didn't have a car when we moved because I had gotten rid of my Camry right before we moved to Pullman, so I had to either walk or take the bus, but back then, the bus service was what one might expect in a farming community. There were about three buses for the whole town, and they stopped once a day at each stop, so that wasn't an option for my crazy schedule. As a result, I walked every-fucking-where, and thanks to the hills and the snow—wait for it—I really did walk uphill in the snow to school. Both ways. And I won't let my kids forget it.

In addition to my many other faults as an arrogant 28-year-old, I was fairly proud of my hair. I styled it carefully and probably spent more time than I should have on getting it right in the mornings, and the sheer amount of product I put in it to keep it that way was probably enough to pave someone's driveway. See, I'm the kind of person who likes control over every element of my persona that others see, so that meant I had to maintain consistency.

This created a serious dilemma. As the temperature dropped, I was faced with yet another impossible choice: either maintain my 'gelmet' or cover it up with a beanie (toque, for all my Canadian friends). Of course, if I covered it with a beanie, then the inevitable result would be hat-hair, and that was simply unacceptable, despite the fact that I had nobody to impress. Initially, I tried dealing with the issue by wearing a beanie all day like a hipster, but my head felt like it was on fire, and trust me, the processing power required by my brain in calculus class necessitated either a built-in heatsink or no hat at all.

My brilliant wife floated the option of picking up a super-cheap pair of electric clippers and simply clipping my hair so short that wearing a hat wouldn't matter. At first, I resisted the idea, thinking it might make me look stupid (these were the post-mullet days where I hadn't fully let go of the Kentucky waterfall yet), but the prospect of paying for haircuts when we were struggling to buy food wasn't sitting well with me either, so I relented. Her idea worked perfectly; I didn't look too terribly ridiculous, and it afforded me the protection I needed from the cold while still allowing my big-ass noggin to breathe in math class. Problem solved.

One day, about a month and a half into our weekly tradition of sitting down for a trim, my wife was clipping my hair using the guard, as usual. I drifted off into a trance, preparing for her to mow my dome, when suddenly, I felt a sharp tug right in the middle of the top of my scalp, accompanied by a muted, "Whoops." This was followed by a stifled, yet uncontrollable giggle from my wife, and I knew exactly what had fucking taken place. Partly due to the cheap nature of our clippers and partly resulting from what I still contend was carelessness (though I've no doubt she'll adamantly deny that portion of the story), the guard fell off right before her initial pass down the middle of my head, which meant that the clippers gave me what can only be described as an inverse Mohawk.

Panic settled in first. At 28, I had never seen my scalp, save for baby pictures, of which there were no more than about 7 or so. I had to be at school and work the following day, and I immediately knew there was only one possibility for remedying this condition: shave the whole fucking thing to match. As my panic intensified, self-judgment showed up next, which led to an absolute dread of what people the next day were going to think of me. I could instantly hear their responses. "Is it cancer?" "How's the lice treatment going?" "Lose a bet?" "How much did Locks of Love give you for the Tennessee Top Hat there, MacGyver?" Of course, the people not making fun of me indirectly would simply think to themselves, *what a douche nozzle*.

The next day, I didn't want to remove my hat. I thought that maybe I could simply wear it until it grew out again, and all would be well with my world. But, something crept up in my mind while I was at work in the university's physics lab. It was a still, small voice in the back of my head that whispered, "Josh, you have nobody to fucking impress. Take off the fucking hat." I did. Guess what? Not a goddamn peep from anyone. That's not totally true. One guy looked at me a couple seconds longer than normal before asking what happened, which gave me the opportunity to tell the story and get the same gut-busting laugh from him that I get from anyone else hearing the story for the first time, including yourself, I hope.

That day, I stood toe-to-toe with my perceptions and realized quickly that they were not perceptions at all; they were fucking delusions. Everyone else around me was so focused on their own shit and their own issues that they had neither the energy nor the desire to notice my seemingly drastic change. I was the only one placing so much importance on my hair, making me question why it had taken nearly 30 goddamn years to arrive at that conclusion. To this day, I still shave the whole fucking thing, and you know what? Each time I take a razor to my scalp, I recall this story with glee. I remember how wonderful it felt for those delusions to crash down around me, liberating me from my self-imposed limitations.

### Public Pajama Party

My second story of confronting delusions arrived a significant amount of time after the shaving incident, making it even more worthwhile to examine, because one would think I'd learned my lesson from the inverse mohawk, but such was not the case. It was shortly after I had graduated with my master's degree and started teaching. As a result of the newfound importance and prestige I had been awarded by my position, I tried to elevate my personal appearance standards as well. In my mind, professors wore tweed or corduroy jackets with suede patches on the sleeves, Carl Sagan-esque turtlenecks, slacks, and penny loafers. I never took it that far (thankfully), but I figured that, anytime I was out in public, I needed to look like a professor to maintain that image because one never knows when a student or another prof might show up in the produce aisle.

The day in question was a typical sick day. Everyone in my family—wife, kids, myself—had come down with a nasty bug, and we were all in the process of resting it out while binging our favorite old TV show, which featured a meth-cooking high school chemistry teacher. Later that day, we needed to re-up our sick day supplies, which included crackers, chicken noodle soup, and of course, everyone's favorite, nighttime sleepy meds. Unfortunately, I drew the short straw and was the elected family representative tasked with the mission of retrieving said supplies for the rest of the team.

Upon this decision, I retreated to the bedroom and started rummaging through my dresser for a pair of jeans when Stacie, my wife, walked in and asked, "What the fuck, Josh?" I explained that I was getting dressed because I wasn't about to go to the store in my pajamas, to which she replied, "Why the hell not?"

Damn. Good question, dear. But, I couldn't let her be right yet again. Not after the whole 3-P incident from Chapter 2. "I'm changing because I don't want to run into a student and have them see me in my jammies, that's why."

She then gave me the classic look, peering over her glasses at me, and said, "Seriously? Why change just to change back again 10 minutes later? Get over yourself." I love my wife's penchant for blunt honesty. What she knew about me that I didn't, despite my knowledge of the blind spot and how all this bullshit works, was that I still had a trace of old Josh in me, the one who needed to manicure his appearance and constantly manipulate public perception of himself. She also recognized that the trace of old Josh still left behind also still had a pretty sizable ego, so she punctuated her response by *daring* me to go to the store in my pajamas and hoodie.

Here's the thing: I don't back down from dares, especially from her. As I walked toward the store, I pulled my hood down over my face, hoping to hide my identity in case I saw anyone I knew, especially a student. I tried being incognito as possible while I walked across the busy parking lot, but then I realized something. Nobody noticed. Nobody fucking cared. There were no pointing fingers, no children laughing, and no muffled giggles. I ended up running into a former student, who asked how I was doing, listened as I complained about coming down with the Black Death, and wished me well without even so much as a snide "Nice pants, Misner." Once again, not a single fucking person noticed or seemed to care. My perceptions were delusions, and the only one heaping standards upon my shoulders was me.

Today, years later, when this chapter challenge comes up as an activity in my college courses, I wear my pajamas to campus. I've even attended college senate meetings with deans and vice presidents present while wearing my favorite My Little Pony jammies that my daughter made me buy. Each time I do, I continue to chip away, piece by laborious fucking piece, at my ego, realizing ever so slowly that I really don't have anyone to impress, like the still, small voice in the back of my mind suggested to me all those years ago.

It's high time we start confronting our erroneously assumed and self-imposed judgments to give ourselves permission to let go of that anxiety to enjoy the most life has to offer. Of course, that's never going to happen if we don't put the fucking phone down and challenge ourselves to face that fear.

### Chapter Challenge: Reckless Within Reason

Our challenge this go-round is simple to explain, yet, so painfully difficult to put into action. Remember the question from the beginning of the chapter? You guessed it, go do that motherfucking thing. Challenge yourself to do something (legal) in public that you normally wouldn't do out of fear of others' judgment. Make it a good one, because the harder you challenge yourself, the bigger the payoff will be. If you need some ideas from what others have tried in the past, here you go:

- Go to work/school/shopping in your pajamas;
- Sing karaoke (bonus points for doing it sober);
- Go dancing and really get into that shit;
- Perform an original poetry reading at an open mic night;
- Grab your child's hand and skip through the store while singing, "We're off to see the wizard" at the top of your lungs with reckless abandon;

- While out with friends, choose one of the following highly immature activities:
    - Vehicular Musical Chairs: At a red light, everyone in the car jumps out, takes a lap around the car, and gets back in, not necessarily in the original seating configuration;
    - The Floor is Lava: Whenever someone shouts, "the floor is lava," everyone in the vicinity must leap off the floor and onto anything else;
    - Polar Plunge: Jump into the nearest water, fully clothed. The colder the water, the higher the degree of difficulty;
- Ask out that secret crush you've been admiring, and fucking own that shit like it was meant to be;
- Join a gym and start taking cardio classes, particularly those that involve dancing;
- Join an intramural sport, especially if nobody you know is taking part, like dodgeball, softball, basketball, or billiards.

Better yet, do ALL these and more! With the degree of liberation one feels as they take part in the fun, it can become addictive, and before you know what's happened, you have a newfound confidence, absolutely NONE of which is dependent upon battery life, Wi-Fi signal strength, or screen resolution.

As you engage in these activities, take time to focus on how it feels before, during and afterward. Before, you likely feel the pangs of anxiety and worry. During, you will probably notice those feelings dissipating and the weight of that burden lifting. Afterward, you may feel elated, joyful, and alive. But, pay close attention to how these evolving emotional states unfold. Focus on being reckless within reason, as the title implies. Push the boundaries of your comfort zone, little by little initially, and then go fucking nuts with it whenever you're ready (legally, of course). Pushing those boundaries is amazingly good for us, as it builds confidence, self-esteem, and ultimately, helps us learn to put the fucking phone down and live life for once. Instead of hiding behind a screen, we can learn to confront life as it happens, taking the good with the bad, all while opening ourselves up to more and more opportunity.

In the next chapter, we're going to capitalize off that newfound freedom and confidence, so go out and practice now. Come back to the reading only when you're ready to see where that can take us.

# 6

## BEING WRONG IS OH-SO-RIGHT

In the most-viewed TED talk of all time (as of the writing of this book), Sir Ken Robinson famously stated:

> *Kids will take a chance. If they don't know, they'll have a go. Am I right? They're not frightened of being wrong. I don't mean to say that being wrong is the same thing as being creative. What we do know is, if you're not prepared to be wrong, you'll never come up with anything original — if you're not prepared to be wrong. And by the time they get to be adults, most kids have lost that capacity. They have become frightened of being wrong. And we run our companies like this. We stigmatize mistakes. And we're now running national education systems where mistakes are the worst thing you can make.*

Not all that long ago, my wife bravely confronted me about my phone usage, which should probably have been labeled an addiction. She wasn't exactly gentle with her words, as I seem to recall her saying something about how I live life with my phone in my face. When she first pointed it out, my first instinct was to react by telling her how wrong she was. And, of course I did, because that strategy worked so well for me in the past. We obviously know the outcome of that insanely fucking stupid response, because here we are, reading a book about putting down the fucking phone.

I look back on that situation and quite possibly hundreds of others like it, and this reflection leads us to a shiny, brand-new question: what the actual fuck was I thinking? To be more specific, I ask myself why I was so reactive, not only in this context but also in so many others. Anytime someone attempted to explain how I was wrong, mistaken, confused, or simply flat-out full of shit, my natural instinct was to defend myself. I've seen this same behavior in hundreds, if not thousands, of others as well. I've listened to students complain about their partners, friends, parents, in-laws, and other people important to their lives, stating that these other people clearly had a phone addiction and couldn't manage to live through more than five fucking minutes of interaction before whipping out their little black boxes and scrolling away mindlessly and endlessly.

Let's start by examining the situation further, and if you find yourself in a similar one, perhaps by me tracing my way through our interaction, it may shed some new insight for you as well. It all started with the nature of the relationship itself: I was interacting with my wife, my partner, and one of the most important people in the world to me, so I obviously value what she thinks of me more than nearly any other human, save for my children. If she thinks less of me, reflecting back to the idea of the looking glass self from Chapter 4, then by proxy, I would think less of myself.

Not if she's wrong!

If I could have convinced not only myself, but also my wife that she was wrong, then nothing about my self-perception would change, leaving merely an anomaly as a blip on the radar for our relationship. That's some shady-ass Walter White shit, right there. However, I think a lot of us do exactly this same thing on a regular basis because I've witnessed it as a bystander—frequently. We defend ourselves from having others—especially those who are important to us—think we're wrong or somehow less-than. We don't want those who are important to us to think less of us, but we also don't want to think less of ourselves as a result, and that's pretty fucked up.

Now, let's look at another question, and I wager this one is even more important: What in the hallowed blistering hell is so bad about being wrong that anyone would resort to manipulative and devious behavior like this? Let's pretend that, in my situation, I approached the outcome differently.

Stacie: "Josh, you have a problem. Seriously, it's like you live life through that tiny screen, and it's getting really fucking annoying, especially when you don't listen to anyone and forget even the simplest grocery lists."

Me: "Shit, really? I didn't realize it was getting that bad or that I was making you feel that way. I'm sorry. I'll try to work on it. Will you forgive me?"

It doesn't take a rocket surgeon to predict the outcome of this hypothetical situation. Not only is there pretty much zero chance of the conflict train showing up unannounced to take me on a trip to sleep-on-the-fucking-couch town, but if I had actually reacted like that, I probably would have earned my wife's respect, I would have become a better role model to my kids, and I would have given myself a big step toward my own personal development. The first reaction (the one that actually took place) made me out to be a total dick, concerned only with his self-image and being right at any cost, and I'm reasonably certain that's how my wife perceived me when it happened. The second, more hypothetical reaction makes me out to be kind, caring, compassionate, and actually concerned with how others feel. It represents the kind of person I'd like to be perceived as, and that's also the kind of person I'd want to hang out with, which begs the question, why the fuck don't I act like that more often? I think we all know the answer here, and it starts with the ego, as well as an incessant need to defend it.

In Chapter 5, I proposed that we try being reckless within reason, to push the boundaries of our comfort zones with the goal of doing something we normally wouldn't for fear of how others might judge us. In doing so, the goal was to feel *alive*, throwing off the bondage of our self-imposed limitations to further liberate ourselves through the pursuit of valuable life experiences. I'm sure you can predict where this is heading, because it's time for us to tap into that courage for an even more valuable endeavor. But first, let's talk cats and dogs.

Never, in a million years, did I think I would end up a cat person, but here I am, surrogate human to an annoying-as-fuck orange tabby called Buttercup. She's such a bitch. I know that's more of a term for a dog, but I don't know what word means 'cat with a shitty attitude' other than merely 'cat.' Perhaps such attitude is already embedded.

Pet her the wrong way or at the wrong time, and she'll release your blood from the skin prison of your body in a hurry. Pet her the right way and stop, and she'll start biting you exactly hard enough to let you know that you're not done, and she needs more attention. Valuable tchotchkes must never sit within 12 inches of a ledge of any kind, else they succumb to gravity by way of a mischievous swipe.

None of this differentiates her from any other cat; sure, she's a bitch, but she's also a prototypical feline bitch (please don't mind either my redundancy or repetitiveness). With all this complaining, one might question my affinity for this 10-inch-tall fur-bearing queen of the realm, but the reason is simple: I admire her inherent feline qualities. She doesn't blindly dole out affection; her adoration has to be earned via a long-term payment plan. It took years of playing the long game to get her to cuddle on my lap for five minutes a day. In a sick sort of way, I see a piece of myself in Buttercup: somewhat shy, reserved, or even standoffish at first, guarded, and untrusting, and I carefully select whom I choose to allow into my "circle of trust," as Jack mused in *Meet the Parents*.

That stated, I tend to view dogs suspiciously, with an air of near-condescension. Let's admit it openly – dogs are stupid. Before anyone crucifies me and takes to social media to complain about what an animal-hating shitbag I am, keep reading, and ponder my argument. Dogs offer almost completely blind loyalty to not only their people, but *any* people in most cases. Give a dog a bit of food—not even good food, mind you—a belly rub, or some positive attention, and that dog becomes the canine equivalent of a long lost relative. Once we've earned this trust, we can toss invisible treats, and they'll lunge for them. We can leave them alone, either all day or for five minutes, and they're at the door when we walk in, acting like we were gone for years. We can skip a feeding, and they don't complain. We can forget to refill the water bowl, and they'll cheerily head to the toilet without complaint. Regardless of our indiscretions, a dog's blind loyalty remains unwavering.

My wife is the primary dog person in our house, and she's brainwashed our children, recruiting them into her canine army, leaving me as the sole rebellious cat aficionado. Everyone else in our house abso-fucking-lutely adores dogs, so we've always had at least one (more often, three). Throughout the tenure of our family's diverse pet relationships, I've had plenty of time to compare and contrast, which has afforded me the analogy I use here: Cats represent everything I currently am, while dogs represent the way I should be more often.

Piss off a cat, and she'll never fucking forget it. Cats hold grudges for life. I know this from bitter experience after teasing my mom's cat as a kid. I went to her house to do my laundry as a 20-something, and that cat *still* fucking hated me enough to swipe at my feet from under the door like she was trying to render my Achilles tendon in twain, and all I did was scare her once – when I was only 10 fucking years old. Our beloved Buttercup frequently scavenges for goodies in kitchen cabinets when left open, and when I catch her in the act, I have to be mindful of *how* I catch her, because if I scold or scare her too badly, she'll turn on me, and months pass before she lets it go.

It wasn't until recently that I came to the realization that this is me. When someone makes a sarcastic or flippant comment that gets under my skin, I will wrestle that fucking comment to the ground and grapple with it for at least a week. I have won more imaginary arguments in my shower that way than I care to even discuss. I juggle every last possible variation of shoulda, woulda, coulda until I have covered up the memory of that comment like my cat buries her turd biscuits in the pooey-box.

Dogs, on the other hand, don't seem to have the mental capacity for grudges. Either that, or they are genuinely and intrinsically goodhearted. The cat person in me votes for the former, while I'm sure my family would smack me and suggest the latter holds true. For example, our gargantuan yellow lab named Tommy Boy, who was clearly blessed with size over brains (hence the unironic name), gets himself into a lot of trouble, most of which involves leveraging his freakishly mutated height to consume partial sticks of butter left out on the kitchen counter. Of course, when this happens, he is loudly reprimanded, at which point, he smiles (yes, really), puts his baseball bat of a tail between his legs, and retreats to his doggy bed. For the next 30 seconds, he shows remorse by perpetuating the cheesy smile, and by the tick of the next minute, his memory resets, and he approaches me, angling for a belly rub, already having let go of the scolding.

Here's the thing: both animals were clearly in the wrong within their respective contexts. The real difference is in how each one reacted to having been confronted, which leads me to ask myself, do I really want to be like a cat and ruminate on everything, or do I want to emulate a dog and let things go more readily? If I continue behaving like Buttercup, then I'm going to waste a shitload of my life trying to resist change in a futile attempt at ignoring each and every time I'm wrong. If, on the other hand, I adopt Tommy Boy's behavior, then I'm much more likely to take an honest approach to being wrong, admit fault openly, and actually fucking learn from my mistakes, freeing up a hefty and significant amount of my life to move on to more worthwhile endeavors.

Consider the impact such a change could have on others. I mean, when Buttercup does something wrong, I ruminate over her misdeeds almost as much as she dwells on the way I yelled at her. Both of us end up trapped in a cycle of replaying the incident in our minds, allowing it to take up rent-free residence. When Tommy Boy lets go and seeks redemption, his actions disarm me, thereby giving me permission to let go as well. Through his act of letting go (even if his actions are the result of an apparent lack of grey matter), it sets a precedent for me to let go as well.

There's a clear connection between this chapter's content and the last chapter. We avoid admission of fault because we're so often afraid of what others might think of us if we admit when we're wrong. That's where challenging our comfort zones comes into play. This chapter's challenge involves thinking of something we did wrong and seeking redemption for it as a means of breaking down these self-imposed barriers. Before we get to that, let's step back and examine the process of redemption. Seeking redemption through admission of fault can be tricky, but at its most basic, involves three seemingly simple steps:

1. Initiate reconciliation;
2. Admit fault;
3. Complete reconciliation by requesting forgiveness.

And here is an alternative list of activities, each of which is considerably more attractive than the process outlined above:

- Root canal;
- Colonoscopy;
- Tax audit;
- Full body wax;
- Waiting in line for a theme park ride;
- Jury duty;
- Comprehensive final exams.

There's no getting around it; redemption isn't at all comfortable. However, as we pursue redemption more frequently, we begin to experience the benefits of doing so, which makes the process considerably easier and more rewarding.

**Step 1: Initiate reconciliation**

Stepping up and being the first person to initiate reconciliation, especially when doing so involves being the first to admit fault, is no simple feat. In most cases, it's goddamn daunting. All too often, we want to feel justified by bathing in self-righteous indignation, or we don't want to lose face by stepping up first, especially us dudes, who fear appearing weak. We want to win, and that's precisely where the first big-ass mistake resides. Unless a conflict is taking place on a field with a ball, presided over by a referee, and sanctioned by a league, then there are no fucking winners or losers! When a conflict is resolved to everyone's satisfaction through a process of compromise, then regardless of how that resolution takes place, everyone wins. The only time there are losers in a conflict are those with no resolution, in which case, everyone loses once the relationship is dissolved over the root cause.

Take a moment to think of the peacemakers in our lives. We all know them – the people who are always the first to speak up, calm one another down, and act as the voice of reason amid the chaos. How do we perceive these people? Are they weak? I'd wager most of us are like me, and I view those people as cool-headed, strong communicators, not to mention the precise kind of people I look up to — anything BUT weak. The person who steps up first is neither weak nor a loser. That person is a leader.

**Step 2: Admit fault**

Once we've initiated reconciliation, it may be tempting to start placing blame and pointing fingers to shift or share in the burden of discomfort, but the most important step is to own our role in the conflict and admit where we are wrong without such a shift. Think of this as the "I'm sorry" portion of the process. Even if I think the other person is being a complete and utter assclown, I need to be the bigger person and own *my* role and mine alone. It's tough to avoid backhanded accountability, where we admit fault but then tie that admission to something the other person did. For example: "I'm sorry I've been absorbed in my phone so much, but truth is, you've been pretty fucking boring lately."

Yeah, that's not going to go over well.

For real, leave off any *but* statements. They're generally a bad idea. It's best to own our part in the conflict alone, which then gives the other person the potential to own her or his part in the conflict. It's much easier for us to follow someone's lead and admit our own faults than it is to be told we're wrong. Reciprocation is a powerful interpersonal communication tool, but we have to trust the other person enough to do so on her or his own without forcing it.

How often do most of us stop there? "I was wrong. I'm sorry." Then, nothing else. This might seem like a trivial point, but the third step that follows here is a critically important one to use. It's also the toughest.

### Step 3: Request forgiveness

"I'm sorry" does little more than simply admit guilt. Admitting guilt and owning our faults is a great step toward reconciliation, but it's incomplete. Forgiveness, at its core, is the act of accepting that the past cannot be changed and subsequently, thereby mutually letting go. By taking the extra step of seeking forgiveness, we are asking the other person to accept us as-is, even though we may have committed the faults we previously owned. This is potentially fucking terrifying, because it temporarily places the other person in a position of power over us. What if the other person responds by saying no? That moment is humbling AF, because rejection stings. In most cases, however (major transgressions notwithstanding), the other person almost predictably grants forgiveness, which transforms the humility gamble into downright elation, bringing both parties back into kumba-fucking-ya harmony with one another. This delicate dance of dialogue won't happen, however, if we can't learn to put the fucking phone down and practice being brave with our most important relationships.

### Chapter Challenge: Let Go Like Fido

Remember earlier, when I mentioned that we were going to tap into some of that newfound courage we developed from last chapter's challenge? It's fucking go-time.

First up, identify a shitty thing you did to someone else, and don't weasel out of this one because you think you're a really great person. Odds are, it probably involves staring into a fucking phone, which is the whole reason we're here. If you can't think of something, ask a good friend or family member. Remember the Blind Spot activity? As you identify this transgression, examine the roots of the situation and each detail of your involvement. How did you inflame the situation? What motivated you to be such a shithead? Perhaps you didn't know you were being a shithead, so how did you become aware of your alleged shitiness, and when you did, how did you react? Trace the roots so you can effectively own every last element.

Second, set up a time to meet with the person you wronged, preferably in-person and over a good meal. Remember, great conversation happens over great food, especially if the time you set aside is reserved for focusing on one another and not our fucking phones. In fact, leave the fucking phone in the car or something. Remove all temptation.

Third, during your meal with this person, review the conflict—not pointing out the other person's role at all—and then seize on the opportunity to completely and fully own your faults as previously identified. Once you have fully admitted to your role in the situation, apologize and most importantly, request forgiveness, fully prepared to absorb the awkwardness and fear that comes with doing so.

The situation you choose could be significant and life-altering, such as restoring a relationship that has remained idle or withdrawn for too long, but you can also start smaller in scope, such as asking forgiveness from a roommate for stealing the last of the chips during a half-asleep late-night binge or reconciling with your child after yelling at her for that time she interrupted to share her latest artwork with you. Perhaps even consider seeking forgiveness from your parents for not calling as often as you should. Sorry, that was a hint to my own kids, should they ever read this book.

After this activity, spend some time in thought. Reflect on why you may have hesitated to seek forgiveness after saying sorry in the past. Dwell on the feelings of elation that come with letting go and moving on. Consider what barriers get in the way of initiating reconciliation, admitting fault, and asking for forgiveness. Imagine what life might look like if we cleared out those barriers. Think carefully about how it felt in this activity to let go and release yourself from your ego as the act of reconciliation took place.

**Story Time!**

I attended private Christian school up until fifth grade. It was actually nothing more than a group of kids of varied ages all homeschooling under the same roof, so it wasn't technically a private school by the strictest definition, but suffice it to state that I was not well socialized before entering the lair of heathens that was public elementary school.

The year was about 1985, and I was really fucking desperate for friends. I was the most awkward kid you've probably ever seen, although I prided myself on being a social chameleon who could blend in just about anywhere, so I was working hard on developing a reputation as a cool kid. One snowy winter day in particular, I was leaving school when I saw a group of popular kids standing on a sidewalk kiddy-corner from my school, and on the corner across from them stood an outcast. You know the type — didn't shower often, smelled a bit funny, greasy, long hair, and generally kept to himself.

I don't know what manner of hell-spawn possessed me that afternoon, but I crossed the street, walked up to this kid, and shoved him down in the snow. I called him names loudly enough to get the attention of the popular kids I so desperately wanted to be friends with, but as I did so, the outcast only looked back at me in bewilderment. I'll never forget his look. It was an expression that made me want to wink at him and somehow tell him I only needed him to play along so I could impress the others. But, I didn't.

Instead, as the outcast stood up, brushing the snow off his dirty black jeans, I walked up and threw the first and only punch of my life, and it connected square to his left cheek. His head rocked back, and he stumbled a bit. "Come on, dude!" I egged him on, "Do something!" That's when I saw the small drips of crimson melting the snow below his face. He looked up at me as if to ask why I would do something as horrific as this, and when I looked across the street at the popular kids, their faces expressed the same confusion. I felt as though I was having an out-of-body experience and watching myself do this absolutely atrocious thing to a young man who clearly never did anything to deserve it, but I continued. I put him in a headlock and choked him with my pre-teen rage as he struggled to get free. Eventually, he broke my grasp on his neck and fell to the snow, sobbing. At that moment, I collected myself in silence, turned in shame, and ran away.

For the rest of that year, the outcast never looked me in the eye. He always sat on the opposite side of the lunch room, played on the opposite kickball team, and generally avoided my presence. The more distance between us, the more I longed to apologize and beg him for forgiveness, but the more time I allowed to pass, the harder that act became. After sixth grade, we all diverged paths to various junior high schools, and later I found out that the outcast attended an alternative school for kids with unique life situations. In other words, he went to the school where all the burnouts, stoners, and pregnant girls ended up, and part of me wondered if that was my fault.

Not a year passed without thinking about what I'd done, which was always accompanied by a yearning to make things right somehow, but I didn't know what happened to him or even how to go about contacting him. The shame wore heavy like a lead backpack I couldn't remove. I especially thought of the outcast when I landed my first teaching job at the very same alternative school he had attended, where my perception of the kids attending that school changed dramatically after helping a young teenage mother land a scholarship to Harvard.

Eventually, I started teaching about the need to seek forgiveness, and I remember telling this story to my students, at which point, someone pointed out the power of social media, and a light bulb shone right into my fucking eyes. Why in the holy fucking hell hadn't I thought of this before, I asked myself? After class, I looked up the outcast on Facebook and found him immediately. I learned he had a family and worked as an automotive service tech, living a seemingly great life in Arizona.

That was the moment I knew I had to make things right again.

I composed a lengthy message that I edited for at least an hour. I told him that he may or may not remember me, but I recounted what I did that day and how it continued to haunt me, well into my late thirties. However, instead of somehow placing the burden on him to reconcile, I took full responsibility and gave him the option of not having to reply by telling him that I simply needed to ask forgiveness, stressing that he was not obligated in any way to respond. My finger hovered above the "Send" icon for what seemed like an eternity before I finally said "Fuck it" and clicked. Then, I waited, watching for a read receipt like a fucking osprey.

Then, I saw it: those three dancing bubbles on the screen letting me know he was responding. I went into full-on holy-shit panic mode, wondering what he would say in response. Would he remember? What if he told me that I'd fucked him up and he needed years of therapy to get over it? How would I deal with that kind of rejection, as Marty McFly would say? Minutes passed, but they felt like hours, though eventually, his response came through.

He confessed to not remembering the incident in question but also explained that it was one of many. He also told me that, at that time in his life, his old man beat the living shit out of him on a daily basis, so he'd learned how to take a beating. This was followed up by confessing that he acted the same way quite frequently and had to deal with a lot of those memories later on, in adulthood, before starting his own family. Ultimately, he accepted my apology and told me he appreciated that I'd sought his forgiveness, and when I read that, I fucking wept.

Today, we're friends. The act of accountability and seeking forgiveness removed the weight of a 1952 Buick from my shoulders that I had unnecessarily carried around for the better part of my life, and although I needed to communicate with the outcast via social media, this would have never happened if I'd merely zoned out. Putting the fucking phone down and owning my mistakes was one of the best decisions I'd ever made.

# 7

# THE DREADED V-WORD

Okay, we've tap-danced our way around the v-word long enough. It's time to confront that dreaded scourge of the relational world: vulnerability. Cue the scary music, right? Vulnerability is the state of being exposed to the potential for being attacked or harmed, regardless of whether this is in a physical or emotional sense. I don't know about you, but reading that definition does abso-fucking-lutely nothing for me to understand what it feels like. Instead, let's list off some of the more common situations marinated in this state of discomfort and fear:

- The moment I realize it's my turn to speak in public;
- Locking eyes with a blind date for the first time;
- The seconds before vocalizing those three little words for the first time;
- Disrobing at a public beach;
- Asking that attractive someone out for the first time;

I could go on, but I'm sure you get the point. To be vulnerable is to bathe in unsettlingly frigid uncertainty and expect ourselves not to shiver. Being vulnerable exposes ourselves to the potential to endure ridicule, shame, embarrassment, humiliation, and an overflowing fuck-load of other shit most of us would much rather avoid.

Most of us, particularly those of the male variety, tend to think of vulnerability as the exact opposite of strength. After all, if vulnerability exposes us to attack, then wouldn't being vulnerable make us weak, overly sensitive, afraid, or fragile? Vulnerability is all too often conflated with submissiveness, like a dog rolling over to bare her belly, so we tend to associate the v-word with a lack of confidence, fear, and being timid. My theory is that those who shun vulnerability by calling it weakness do so because they're incredibly fucking terrified of it. It's far easier to dismiss being vulnerable as weakness than to try to confront and understand it in all its complexity.

Anyone who has ever been in a mature, nurturing, long-term relationship with another human—whether family, friends, or love interests—knows that, to invest in the relationship and take it to a deeper level means to open oneself up to the potential for rejection. That's why we feel that dull thud land in our stomachs the moment before we say those three little words for the first time. What if they don't love me back? Will they love me the same way I love them, and worse, if they don't, then what does that say about me? Falling in love and committing to another person carries an inherently ever-present risk, and the deeper we love, the more potential that risk has for an equivalent or perhaps even greater amount of pain. Sure, most of us would cry if we saw a dog dying, but what if that was the family dog with whom we'd created 10-15 years of memories? Then, we'd have real waterworks flooding our cheeks. In the end, vulnerability is the grand culmination of all our uncertainties and what-ifs, and for many, that, by itself, is terrifying enough to avoid and prevent us from allowing ourselves to be vulnerable.

This brings us to exploring what the hell the v-word has to do with putting the fucking phone down. Here's a hint: It's probably a lot more than you may realize.

A current manifestation of this avoidance is seen with the concept of *phubbing*, or "phone snubbing." Basically, this is when we pull out our phones and bury our faces in these tiny fucking screens as a means of trying to discourage others from interacting, particularly strangers. Take a look at any public queue. Watch students waiting for class to begin. Watch coworkers on their breaks. Scan the audience at your next sporting event or concert before it begins (or possibly during). Regardless of context, there you will see dozens, hundreds, or even thousands of other humans, all avoiding interaction with one another by absorbing the soft glow of their high-resolution screens.

Interacting with strangers is particularly vulnerable because of the high level of uncertainty that comes with it, but some of the most interesting people I've ever met were also those with whom I had abso-fucking-lutely nothing in common and no initial impetus for interaction. In each situation, somebody took a chance and started a conversation, which, of course, provides all parties with the opportunity to do the awkward little dance of stories, sharing one anecdote after another as we compare life experiences to break down the barriers of uncertainty with one another. In doing so, we practice our communication and negotiation skills, we expand our actual social network (as opposed to the virtual one), and the dopamine rewards our brains dole out are significantly greater than those we would have experienced by doing this little dance within the online realm. Such interactions have all the benefits, so why don't we do it more often?

Simply put, we're scared. All that uncertainty causes us to freeze—to paralyze—and, in a panic, we reach for the sole source of comfort we can think of in an instant: our phone. What would happen if we resisted that distraction and gave real interaction a shot once in a while? Perhaps we'd run into some shady characters who started rattling off conspiracy theories or professed their love for fungi, or maybe we'd run into people who are equally scared shitless of vulnerability, people who tell us to fuck right off and leave them alone. Those are the risks we take, but even stories with less than amicable endings provide interesting fodder for the tales we tell our loved ones later.

### Vulnerability's Cousin: Accountability

We've established that to be vulnerable is to expose ourselves to potential ridicule. Part of that property often involves admitting fault, which we covered at length in Chapter 6, so I won't rehash that, but to fully explore what it means to practice vulnerability, we have to examine what it means to take accountability. Remember that story way back in Chapter 4, the one that ended up with the realization that everyone thought I was an asshole? Around that time, as I've mentioned before, I fucking hated being wrong, and more than that, I hated when others *thought* I was wrong. To me, being perceived as wrong meant being perceived as weak.

After the infamous blind spot incident, I began paying more attention to people in my life who I admired and respected, partly because I was making the intentional choice to learn from those role models and shape my behavior. One of the most immediate lessons I took away from observing good people was that they were always quick to absorb fault, but not in a way that made them seem weak or feeble. Instead, they quickly defused conflict, all while exhibiting a high degree of humility and keen self-awareness.

Often, they would even take blame for things they didn't even fucking do, and they seemed to enjoy doing this as a way of helping others save face, especially when those other people were in a subordinate position, such as employees who directly reported to them at work. By helping others save face, they created a culture of accountability within their organizations, which led to people frequently rushing to take accountability, almost as though doing so awarded a badge of honor. Think about this. Instead of your typical organization, where everyone points fingers at everyone else like spoiled children who don't want to take blame, there were these organizations where fault was practically celebrated openly, and in doing so, they spent less time on detective work and more on addressing potential issues.

I started emulating these behaviors in my personal life, and initially, it seemed to take others by surprise, probably for the sole fact that I was transitioning from full-time asshole to decent-person-in-training. I experimented by admitting to mistakes, even before I was 'caught' for having made them. I approached my college professors and admitted to having made mistakes in my work before they found them. The results of my experiments shocked the holy fucking shit out of me. My professors took a look at my work before everyone else's work, corrected me, and then offered feedback, but here's the real shock: they didn't take off any points for my mistakes. I'm like, what in the glowing fresh hell kind of Kung Fu shit is this, and why is it working? As I started being more open with admitting fault within my marriage, my wife went from being furious AF with my forgetfulness to joking about it how absentminded I am. That's when I discovered the paradox: accountability produces trust and openness in all types of relationships.

. . . as does vulnerability.

What follows is a story of when both came into play for not only me, but the way I raise and teach my children to be in this world. Originally appearing in The Huffington Post (minus all the cursing, because they actually made me behave, so now that it's in my own goddamn book, I can say what I really mean), this story was my first truly viral post. The only reason I mention that is because I've always felt that there's something intrinsically valuable about the elements of this story that make it resonate with many for a reason. Deep down, we all know the power that comes with both vulnerability and accountability, and all we need is a gentle push to be braver when it comes to wielding these interpersonal qualities.

### To the Ticket Agent at the Delta Counter

In Chicago, we marveled at the snowfall on the tarmac. Looking out the window, I joked to my teenage daughter, the eldest of my two girls, "Who's gonna shovel all that snow off the wings before we take off?" A little part of me inside grew worried by the minute, because I knew that the harder the snow fell, the better our chances were for a delay.

Sure enough, our delay came. I refused to let it bother me, as I was intentionally trying to demonstrate patience to both my daughter and six-year-old son accompanying me on our trip back home from seeing my oldest son's graduation from Navy boot camp in Great Mistakes (what recruits affectionately call the town of Great Lakes, Illinois). This was a remarkably hard task, considering that, in the last three days, I had acquired a cumulative four hours of sleep. Regardless, I kept cool with an ounce of pure determination, mixed with a dash of stubbornness.

I ended up sleeping through most of the pre-flight delay, as did my children, but it wasn't until about 30 minutes before landing that my panic set in. The flight attendant announced that, because of the delay, we would arrive at 11:00. Looking at the boarding pass for my connecting flight, I saw it was scheduled to take off at 11:02.

Two motherfucking minutes.

Knowing there was no way I would de-plane in time with two children in tow (from the back row of the plane), I gave up and prepared for the worst. However, the flight attendant, overhearing me discuss with the kids that we would miss our connection, announced to the rest of the passengers to let us go first and as such, remain seated until we got by them. She then used her personal Wi-Fi connection to locate our gate, which was in a completely different terminal.

Two goddamn motherfucking minutes.

It was going to be close, but for some strange reason, I thought that if this young woman refused to give up, then I shouldn't either. Summoning my last remaining fragment of tattered determination, we gave it a go.

As we landed, the sound of seat belts unlatching and carry-on bags zipping broke the silence. The flight attendant implored everyone one last time to remain seated and let us off before they turned off the seat belt light. The ding from the light going off might as well have been a fucking starting pistol. As soon as we stood up to commence our rush, so did everyone else. Every last one of the other selfish-ass passengers ignored the attendant's instructions and went about their day, meandering slowly and taking their time to gather bags, put on coats and perform other menial tasks.

We were the last ones off the fucking plane. I officially concluded that people are assholes (as if there was any doubt before).

I felt my rage simmer, seeing the blatant outpouring of selfishness and willful ignorance, and deep down inside, I somehow knew they were doing it on purpose. My determination to make the connection grew by the millisecond though, and as soon as we were out of the gate, the three of us sprinted — or at least, as fast as a six-year-old's legs can run.

Reaching the terminal and seeing our gate within grasp, I felt a glimmer of hope, but that hope dissipated when I realized the jetway door was closed, the reader board had been updated to reflect the next flight assigned to the gate (which wasn't ours) and the seats surrounding the gate were empty.

Two motherfucking goddamn stupid-ass minutes. We missed our bloody flight because of the two minutes we lost because of the selfishness of others. My outrage turned into a full-on grown-up male equivalent of a tantrum — a mantrum, if you will.

I spotted a ticket agent at the desk in front of our gate, and, struggling through gasps to catch my breath, I shouted in his direction, "Excuse me!"

He turned to see, only to turn around again. That bastard ignored me! "Hey!" I shouted again, breathless and exhausted, "Can you help us?"

"Sorry, but I can't help you right now," he responded, turning his back and walking away from the gate and us.

That was it, the proverbial back-breaking straw. My temper boiled over like scalded milk in a pot far too fucking small to contain it, and I lost my shit fully and completely, shouting, "Well, that's just fucking great! How in the fuck are we supposed to get home?"

The agent sped up, but turned his head slightly back toward us and in a hurried matter-of-fact manner, replied, "If you missed your flight, go see the automated service counter between gates C2 and C3!"

Automated service counter? First, we miss our flight because of selfish assholes, then I'm ignored by the only fucking customer service employee I can find, and now, he wants me to use some fucking computerized system to figure out my predicament for myself? "Stupid piece of shit," I muttered in reference to the fleeing agent.

That's when I looked down at my six-year-old, who was looking up at me. Fuck. He wasn't looking for answers to our problem. He wasn't looking at me because I was being loud, self-righteous and assholishly indignant. He was looking at me because he had never encountered a situation like this before in his young life, and he was trying to navigate uncharted waters.

And there was his father, providing him with a precedent. My childish tirade presented a solution to my son's future conflicts when dealing with difficult situations and even more difficult people.

Sure, I found the self-service station, and it took me all of 60 seconds to scan our tickets and print out boarding passes to another flight, four hours later than our original departure. We now had the time to eat lunch, relax for a bit, and most importantly, ponder how I was going to reconcile what I demonstrated for my children.

I needed redemption, and it had to be something they would never forget, so for the next three hours, I simmered and stewed, allowing my anger to lift like a fog that the sun cuts on a cold, clear winter morning. Contemplate as I might, the best course of action I could come up with was a brief lecture on how it isn't right to lose your temper with others when it isn't their fault, but I knew that a lecture would be forgotten moments after our conversation. I needed something that would stick.

Roughly 30 minutes before boarding our new flight, that's when it hit me, and I intentionally chose to do something daring, something that I normally wouldn't have done, and it is something that I will never regret, for the rest of my natural life.

I spotted the original ticket agent, who was working the desk at our gate again. I grabbed my son's hand and said, "Come with me."

"Why, daddy?" he asked as he looked up from playing a game on my phone.

"Come with me," I insisted, "I need you to listen."

He got up, held my hand, and walked with me across the carpet to the desk. There was a line of passengers, and we waited. My heart began thumping against my ribs, and my palms formed a thin film of sweat. When it was our turn, the agent looked up at me and asked, "Can I help you?"

I doubt he recognized me. I approached the desk with my son's hand in mine and said: "Sir, I don't know if you recognize me, but a few hours ago, I was a total dick to you. I cursed you out because you ran off instead of helping us find a new flight after we missed our connection, and that wasn't right. I took my frustration out on you and set a poor example for my children. I want to apologize."

He looked absolutely fucking floored. He was speechless for what felt like forever, and at the moment I was turned to walk away, he spoke up: "I don't know what to say. I didn't hear you use profanity, but I do remember you. At the time, I was trying to locate a medical kit for a woman boarding her plane over at the gate next door, and I was in a rush. I wanted to help, but I was in a hurry to assist the passenger over there. I'm sorry I didn't stop to help."

I became even more ashamed of my actions. I responded, "You have nothing to apologize for. I was in the wrong, and I need to ask forgiveness to show my son that the way I behaved was not right."

Still in disbelief, he responded, "It's fine. I forgive you, and I can't tell you how much I appreciate your apology. You didn't need to do it. In fact, nobody has ever apologized that I can recall, and trust me, we get yelled at a lot. You just made my day. Thank you." He then extended his hand for a handshake, as he said, "My name is Ron."

Grabbing his hand, I replied, "Thanks, Ron. I'm Josh. I hope you have a great rest of your day."

Turning to walk away after giving Ron a smile, I looked down at my son, who was still gripping my hand tightly. He stared up at me, but this time, doe-eyed, with a hint of a smile. I smiled back, tears brimming on my eyelids, and said, "That, kiddo, is doing the right thing. *Always* do the right thing, no matter what."

Five minutes later, Ron called me back to the desk over the PA. After I sat back down, he had looked at the flight manifest and noticed that the three of us were in separate rows, spread out all over the plane. He took the initiative to not only rearrange other people to allow us to sit together as a family, but also moved us to seats with additional legroom.

Forgiveness is a gift of love, an act of beauty that benefits not only the person being asked by way of reconciliation, but also the person requesting it, by way of redemption.

Thanks to snow, a delayed flight and the selfishness of complete assholes, I had the opportunity to make things right and to set in motion a lifetime of redemption for my children. Sure, I could have taken to social media to express my displeasure with Delta on behalf of their passengers. Actually, truth be told, I'm pretty sure I started penning a nasty post before I had my change of heart. Or, I could have asked for a manager and bitched Ron out, projecting all my problems onto him and transforming him into the whipping post for my issues. I could have live-tweeted the whole thing and gotten hundreds of new followers, all of whom had similar experiences in the past.

But I didn't. I chose to put my fucking phone down and invest in a bit of vulnerability to take accountability for my actions so my kids could see their father do something brave. I hope that stuck with them, so that, next time they're faced with something similar, they tell their impulses to fuck right off and, instead, do the right thing, regardless of how uncomfortable it might be.

## Chapter Challenge: Take a Risk

Now that we've: 1) confronted our blind spots, 2) done stupid shit we normally wouldn't and said to hell with others' judgy McJudgment-face, and 3) practiced the art of seeking forgiveness and admitting when we're wrong, it's time to get our vulnerability on! This one comes in two parts:

### *Part One: Emotional Autopsy*

To begin, let's take some time to write out our thoughts and examine them in more detail. Why we do this is important to understand, so allow me to elaborate. When thoughts swirl around in our heads like little clouds of foggy cognition, they have no form. They're about as abstract as it possibly gets since they're a collection of nerve impulses bouncing from one neuron to another. However, when we write our thoughts down, it's like Harry Potter when Dumbledore took his wand and extracted his thoughts with a touch of J. K. Rowling's imagination, combined with all those cool special effects.

We pull those abstract, ethereal things out of our skulls, send them down our forearm muscle and sinew, and we transform them into a real thing with form. Words are physical, and paper is something we can touch and feel. When we re-read our thoughts that we've written down, we re-experience them through our sense of sight, allowing us to reexamine them using a totally different area of our brains. This is possibly the reason why, when we can't remember something to save our fucking lives but then talk about with someone else, we suddenly remember the name of that one actor from that one movie that took us all goddamn day to recall.

So, what do we write? Begin by writing down all your fears regarding vulnerability. What are its risks, in your eyes? How has vulnerability precipitated in various situations in your life recently, and how has it made you feel? What is there to fear about the dreaded v-word? List ALL your fears, even the most irrational ones. Then, start writing down how you feel about accountability, and for fuck's sake, be honest. It does no good to lie to yourself. Nobody will see this but you, and anyone else who accidentally finds it and posts it to Instagram is an asshole. Does admitting fault scare you? How honest are you with yourself? Are there areas you're more honest with yourself than others? Where might you need some extra time and effort? Be as complete and forthright with this reflection as possible.

*Part 2: Speak Up!*

Once you have your shit together from the first part, leave the house, apartment, condo, dorm, or whatever. Go for a walk to nowhere, and place yourself somewhere you'll find other people. Your goal is to interact randomly with five strangers—face to face, not online! By interaction, I'm referring to at least a 2-minute conversation, if not more. Saying "how's it going" to a stranger and then moving along your merry fucking way before listening to the complete response does not count as interaction. Engage five total strangers in meaningful conversation.

But what do I talk about? Odds are astronomically high that I won't be anywhere even remotely near you when you do this. Shit, go to Walmart, and in the candy aisle, ask someone what their favorite candy is and why. That's your opener, so from there, maybe start telling the other person a story from your childhood about your own favorite. Maybe finish that story by asking the other person if their current favorite is the same as when they were a kid. Or, if you go into a McDonald's to buy a soda, strike up a convo with the person behind the counter or go sit next to someone already sitting alone after asking if you can join them.

Sounds pretty scary, right? I'll bet you're actively thinking of skipping this one and continuing on to the next chapter. Or, you're thinking of chucking this book right now in favor of a YouTube/Netflix/Hulu binge. All those knee-jerk reactions are rooted in fear, and you goddamn well know it. It's time to face that fear, put the fucking phone down, and go challenge yourself to do something brave. After all, this is the last chapter and activity of Part 2, the focus for which has been entirely on challenging ourselves to do braver things. I see this activity as the ultimate challenge for a lot of us, but I can almost certainly guarantee you that you'll enjoy it.

In fact, I invite you to share your experiences with me personally. Connect with me via my website (www.joshmisner.com), leave a comment on my Facebook page or comment on one of my YouTube videos about your experience. Even if it ends up going sideways on you, you'll have a wicked fucking story to tell!

You got this. Go do it.

# PART III:

## PUT THE FUCKING PHONE DOWN & ENJOY YOURSELF

Here we are, at the third of four sections, and if you're still reading this, thank you. Actually, thank yourself, because if you've made it this far, it means you actually give a shit about yourself and your relationships. I mentioned before that I arranged this book similar to how I organize one of my favorite of all classes to teach, so if you're anything like my students, then this is the part of the book they affectionately call, *the turn*. Basically, the chapters and activities leading up to this point tend to have an ever-so-slightly darker tone to them. Think about this for a sec—we've asked others what they hate about us, we've admitted fault (on purpose), we've embarrassed the holy living shit out of ourselves, and with the close of Chapter 7, we actually <GASP> talked to other humans!

I get it. That kind of shit takes a toll on a person — even on me, and I've been doing these activities several times a year for the last seven years.

You may ask, what does he mean by 'the turn' here? The turn is when everything becomes kittens, puppies, unicorns, rainbows, and fuzzy cute bullshit like that. Why? Because this is the point where everything we explore is rooted in the science of positive psychology, which is the study of all that makes life worth living. Seriously, can you think of a more fulfilling career than studying shit like happiness, gratitude, mindfulness, savoring, presence, and appreciation? Personally, I can't.

Therefore, this part of the book—also comprised of four chapters—is where we dive headlong into that science and start applying what we know to our lives. In Chapter 8, we look at the science of savoring the best parts of life; in Chapter 9, we look at how to apply that to some of life's most pressing problems; in Chapter 10, we examine how we can take control over our perceptions using the science of gratitude; and when we get to Chapter 11, we'll look at how expressing appreciation becomes a complete game-changer.

To get to the good stuff or the turn, we had to walk through metaphorical fire, so again, I'm glad you're still here. We've learned about increasing our sense of self-awareness, and we've pushed the boundaries of our comfort zones to start tapping into courage that many may not have even realized they had in them. Let's put those qualities to good use now, as we jump into learning how to appreciate life as it happens.

# 8

# THE SCIENCE OF SAVORING

When most of us see the word *savor*, we probably think of food, particularly food that makes us drool down the front of our shirts like starving freaks, which is what happens to me pretty much every time my wife cooks. She's goddamn good. In fact, if we look up the word *savor* in pretty much any dictionary, we'll find that the definitions are all roughly the same: to taste and enjoy good food or drink completely. Perhaps that definition is why I didn't run across this term in relation to how we're planning on using it in this book for a long time.

**Story Time!**

Back in fall of 2008, I embarked on the final leg of my formal education when I enrolled in Gonzaga University's Doctoral Program in Leadership Studies. My intent was to study communication with respect to leadership and to find a way to connect those concepts to the study of mindful presence. If I'm being brutally honest here, I had no fucking clue what I was going to eventually write my greater than 200-page dissertation study on, other than a vague notion of mindfulness and communication. For years, I struggled and wrestled with various topics, and none of them did my passion and ambition justice, until one night when I had a blinding fucking epiphany and decided I wanted to write about the impact of mindfulness on father-child relationships. Being a dad has always been the topmost privilege of my life. Hands down, there is no dispute. Therefore, researching and studying how to be a better father and then sharing that info with others really got my blood pumping.

Problem was, I started out by thinking that what I was going to study was the impact of gratitude on father-child interaction because I always felt grateful for the experience of being with my children. Most of the time, when they weren't being pint-sized assholes, I felt a sense of overwhelming gratitude for their presence in my life, as well as the gratitude I felt for being privy to their growth and development. Some of my favorite moments of all time involved watching my oldest son play guitar, listening to and enjoying new music with my oldest daughter, observing my youngest daughter create art, and taking my youngest son to a construction site so he could sit and watch a giant excavator dig a really big fucking hole. These might be things my kids have forgotten by now, but in each of these moments, I felt a massive and overwhelming rush of emotion that hit me, nearly moving me to tears. The only way I knew how to describe such moments was being grateful.

So, I studied the piss out of gratitude. I spent more than $300 on gratitude books from Amazon and read every last fucking one of them, hoping I'd find that one little morsel of wisdom that would help me articulate what I was feeling.

But, I got flat-out skunked. Every single last one of those books (and more than three dozen scholarly journal articles) said essentially the same fucking thing: gratitude is an emotion we feel when we receive some sort of gift. See, my kids weren't giving me any gifts, other than the gift of their existence and allowing me to share the same airspace with them. That's a serious stretch that no doctoral committee in the world would accept, and I should know: I've been on a few committees. I needed to sort my shit out and find a word or phrase that helped me articulate what was happening to me, and I needed it fast.

That's when a textbook publisher representative showed up in my office. Now, if you're one of those and reading this, take what I'm about to write with a pinch of humor. Publisher reps are like the cheap used car salespeople of the academic world. Some of them are fucking slimy and make me feel like I need a shower after a visit. But, this one? He showed up at the perfect time and had the perfect book for me. He asked how it was going, and at the moment, I lamented my dilemma, getting ready to make the 45-minute drive to Gonzaga from my office to go to class that night. As I explained it to him, hoping that, somehow, by vocalizing my problem, I'd find a new and unique spin on it. No such luck, though. I was still stuck.

But then, he reached into his bag and pulled out a shiny new textbook on positive psychology. "Try this out. You can have it. If it works for you, great!" And then he did something no other rep ever had—he walked away. I'm convinced he wasn't real. He was my sanity's guardian angel, showing up in the nick of time before I lost my shit completely, using the guise of a publisher rep to get my attention. I took the text with me to class that night, and while we were sitting in the classroom before getting started, I cracked the spine to see if it was worth it. As usual, I flipped to the index and looked up *gratitude*, thinking that maybe this book had a slightly different take, but alas, it said the same exact fucking thing as all the rest. Again, I was lost, but only for a few more seconds.

As I scanned the page, I noticed a heading mere millimeters below the section on gratitude: **Savoring**! Excitedly, I immediately recognize the value of the word, so I kept reading, and on the next page, I found exactly what I had been fucking seeking all along: a way to articulate what I experienced with my children. Game fucking on. So, to that textbook rep, whatever your name was (sorry I don't recall, but I was frazzled), you saved my life and launched my career, so thank you.

Savoring is much more than the highly-limited dictionary definition from the start of this chapter. Savoring is what happens when we notice, appreciate, attend to, and prolong positive experiences in our lives. It occurs when we shift our attention from objective reality to our subjective experience of that moment. It happens when we pay attention to and really marinate in how that moment makes us feel. Savoring causes time to slow to a fucking crawl and can render us speechless, cement the memory of a moment, and even cause us to fall in love. If we pinpoint the moment we realize we're in love, even if we have a hard time describing what love is, then what we're experiencing in that moment is most certainly the science of savoring. To break this down further, savoring can be classified into three time-dependent ways of experiencing the concept (anticipation, savoring, and reminiscence), as well as four categories of savoring that each describe different contexts (luxuriating, basking, thanksgiving, and marvel or wonder).

## Temporal Savoring

That heading may make this part sound complex, but it's actually pretty simple. 'Temporal' merely refers to time, and savoring takes three different forms, depending on exactly what we're savoring in relation to *when* it takes place.

Here's a scenario to help explain it. During the summer, my kids usually earn one free pass each to a local amusement park for having read so many books during the school year. These passes are no joke; they're worth about $50 or so each, and they get us unlimited access to an amusement park full of roller coasters, thrill rides, fun, and of course, the epic water park. Needless to say, my kids yearn for our yearly trip during summer break. Even though it hasn't happened yet, my kids savor the mere idea of heading down the water slides and chowing down on carnie fare. And there it is: anticipation, our first form of savoring.

The mind can be a pretty odd thing. Interestingly enough, brain scans show that the same areas of the brain light up like a fucking Christmas tree whether we're enjoying something in the present, anticipating something in the future, or thinking back to something enjoyable from our past. My kids (and probably yours as well if you have them) are certified anticipation experts. Thinking back to around the mid-1980s, I fucking know I was. I'd suggest that kids' ability to anticipate may even outweigh their actual ability to savor something as it happens. They build things up SO much in their minds that I often worry that they'll end up disappointed, but that's an issue for another time, so bookmark that thought. When we anticipate something, we effectively savor the possibility of a good time. Think about how fucking profound this is: We're actually manufacturing happiness for ourselves out of thin air using nothing but our imaginations. In the next chapter, we'll actually take a look at how to exercise this proverbial muscle and make the most out of anticipation.

So, anticipation is savoring something that hasn't yet happened, and savoring is enjoying something that's happening right now. I've already alluded to it, but savoring something that happened in the past is our third temporal type, and we typically call that reminiscence. Obviously, this is one of those experiences that fades over time, but the stronger our ability to savor in the moment and commit the experience of that moment as it happens, the clearer the memory of that moment and the more likely we are to conjure it up again to continue enjoying it, long after it has already passed. As with anticipation, reminiscence is something we'll exercise in the next chapter.

### *Luxuriating*

Okay, this is the legit, stereotypical form of savoring most of us probably think of, and it's the one most closely connected to the literal definition referenced at the beginning of the chapter. To luxuriate is to savor the pleasurable experience derived from a sensory physical experience. Anything we can take in from our five sense is fair game. When I see a shiny Mustang GT500, I take that shit in. When I hear my favorite song playing, I stop the fucking world to savor it for a few minutes before I put that sucker on repeat 42 times in a row. Luxuriating is what happens when we've worked a long AF day in the yard, come inside, swig down a full bottle of Gatorade (or perhaps an ice cold beer), and then take a shower so hot it melts the pain away, along with the three top layers of skin. To luxuriate is to savor sexual release, the smell of fresh coffee first thing in the morning, or snuggling up with a warm blanket on a snowy winter day.

We experience this type of savoring strongest when it stands in stark contrast to its opposites, such as stress or hard physical labor. Luxuriating is an internal response to an external sensation, but its main drawback is that it is highly difficult to prolong, as we tend to grow accustomed to the sensations far too quickly. It's also prone to a process called *habituation*, which is a fancy, high-tech way of saying that, the more often we do it, like a drink or drug, the more of it we need to feel the same effect. If we really want to enhance this form of savoring, remember that idea of stark contrast. Don't simply go to the spa and enjoy a massage. Do some really fucking hard work beforehand. Get stressed out enough to want to murder someone (please stop *prior* to committing murder). Also, seek luxuriation in moderation, because too much can easily push someone over the edge toward hedonism, where, just like a smack addict, you're out there searching for greater and greater pleasures simply to receive the same benefit.

### *Basking*

Okay, so if *savoring* or *luxuriation* conjures up thoughts of lasagna and a back massage (possibly even at the same time – now, there's an idea . . .) like it does for me right now, then what does the word *basking* produce? For me, every time I see it, I think of a turtle sunbathing on a floating log or my kid's leopard gecko resting on a rock under his sun lamp. Sure, those are technically instances of savoring, but not the kind we're looking at here.

### Story Time!

In January of 2018, my youngest son started guitar lessons, once a week, with a family friend. He was only 10, and his guitar teacher was fresh out of high school. I'll admit, I was worried a bit about this teacher's ability to remain patient with my son (because my son can be an asshole sometimes, like any 10-year-old), and I was worried that maybe I was starting him out a bit young, but we pushed on anyway. As the lessons passed, I realized it was going to be difficult for my son, as he constantly needed reminders and a few threats to practice, so when he showed up to his weekly lesson and was asked to show his progress, he always ended up becoming shy and reserved, knowing he couldn't measure up his expectations. As a result, the teacher would (understandably) force him to practice during the lesson, which also meant that I wasted $20 each and every week my son didn't practice.

During one lesson in particular, I could see his teacher growing frustrated, and it was the hardest thing in the world for me to sit there quietly and allow my son to face the consequences. His teacher spoke bluntly, and next thing I knew, I saw the waterworks come to life. My son's eyes brimmed over with tears because, like me, he doesn't like to disappoint others. The teacher's criticism was rightly justified though, and I knew it was a good lesson for my son to learn. Later that night, the teacher texted me an apology for pushing my son to the point of tears, to which I responded by thanking him for holding my son accountable and providing a valuable lesson.

Over the next week, my son practiced so frequently that I thought his fingertips were going to start bleeding. He was more determined than ever to not experience the guilt he felt for "getting caught" for not practicing as much as he knew he should. We showed up to his next lesson, and my son had this wry, devious, shit-eating grin on his face. His teacher asked him to play the song he had been learning, "Beat It" in the style of Fall Out Boy, and without hesitating, my son abso-fucking-lutely shredded it. I will never forget the look on his teacher's face: eyes bugged out, jaw on the floor, and once my son had finished, he shot his arms up in a V and shouted, "YES!"

At that moment, what I felt was the sensation of basking. I was so fucking proud of my son for the struggle he confronted, dealt with, and surpassed. In seeing the pride and shock on his teacher's face, it only amplified what I felt, and I may have even teared up a bit myself, a real Rudy moment.

Basking is an internal response to an external situation, typically related to pride in oneself for an accomplishment or pride in someone close to us, by proxy. This sensation, once noticed, can easily be enhanced or prolonged, especially if we reference others (such as one's favorite basketball team winning a big game and referencing ourselves to the fans of the other team, who leave the arena with their tails between their legs), reference our current state to our past (such as earning a promotion, reaching a difficult goal, achieving a new personal best, or showing someone who's the fucking boss), or upon flattery.

There is a dark side to basking, however. Too much, and others will interpret our savoring as arrogance or egoism, particularly if our basking is not proportional to the context, or if we do it too frequently. We often resist the act of basking out of fear of others' judgment, which, after the activity from Chapter 5, I hope y'all say "fuck it" once in a while and celebrate yours and others' accomplishments freely.

### *Thanksgiving/Gratitude*

Okay, this one is stupid-easy. This is the type of savoring where we feel that overwhelming sense of thankfulness for something we received. Wow, so complex, right? Hey, at least you didn't have to spend 300 fucking bucks to figure that out, so savor that gratitude for a while. We're going to look much closer at this one in Chapters 10 and 11. On the dark side of gratitude, interestingly enough, it can potentially produce feelings of guilt, indebtedness, and even powerlessness by reminding us of our station in life.

### *Marvel/Wonder*

I deliberately chose to save my fave for last, because this is the type of savoring that was taking place when I was with my kids, not to mention that I feel like this is, by far, the most profoundly powerful form of savoring, while also the hardest to create or seek out. To marvel is to be rendered fully and completely speechless with awe and filled with wonder. It is to be astonished at the ineffable, to feel small and powerless in the sight of something greater than ourselves.

Whoa.

Holy shit.

Louie Schwartzberg, in his TED talk on gratitude, discussed the origin or meaning of the phrase, "Oh my god." He suggested the "oh" represents something that shakes us out of our routine, grabbing us by surprise. The "my" is when we find personal connection to whatever we're marveling at, and the "god" is that feeling of something transpersonal or significantly greater than ourselves. What's funny about this is that "Oh my god" tends to be the go-to phrase for most of us — whether we're religious or not — when we experience marvel or wonder, that is, if we say anything at all. Being wonderstruck is a profound experience that tends to cause the world to melt away, leaving only us and the experience that creates the awe.

For me, every time I was struck with a profound sense of awe when I was with my children, it was usually a time when I suddenly felt so taken by love for these crazy little creatures running around all over the place, and I found it difficult to believe I was that fortunate to be a witness (as well as an active participant) to their growth and development. However, perhaps not all parents feel the way I do about kids, and there's a whole lot of non-parents out there, so let's look at some other examples:

- Holding a newborn baby (yours or not) and recognizing both the fragility and beauty of life;
- Witnessing a musical or other artistic performance that moves one to tears;
- That moment I was hiking in Banff when I came around a corner and saw the bright fucking turquoise water of a glacial lake for the first time, and I didn't even know such a color was possible;
- Those still, peaceful moments without words that we spend with our loved ones, where the world disappears and emotions overtake the need for words.

Sadly, marvel and wonder is fleeting, and it is one of the only types of savoring we cannot effectively create through choice. It won't happen if we are not mindfully present enough to notice such moments, so we can definitely till the soil and make it fertile enough to reap the rewards of marveling, but it can't be forced, which is one of the reasons that makes its experience so fucking insanely powerful.

For marvel to take place, we need to satisfy two conditions: vastness and accommodation. Vastness is the quality in a moment where we recognize something as being significantly greater than ourselves or so fucking far outside the ordinary that we immediately recognize it as a once-in-a-lifetime experience. Accommodation references that for which it is impossible to make sense or understand. When we accommodate an experience in this manner, it forces us to stop and attempt to reach a new understanding of what we're experiencing (remember this as one of the four components of mindful presence?) and why it makes us feel so tiny, insignificant, and inspired. Sometimes, if we try but can't accommodate, it has the potential to leave us feeling terrified, as awe gives way to the fear of experiencing that which we have no capacity for understanding.

Marveling often results in a torrential flood of really fucking powerful emotions: fear, amazement, confusion, empowerment, optimism, and maybe even dread. As a result, this leads to the most powerful and yet, shortest-lived form of savoring, and it also is the most vulnerable form to habituation. Think dulling the senses here. We can only see so many fabulous Waikiki sunsets before it becomes meh. We can only hold our firstborn child for the first time once. There is no kiss like the first one, etc. Sometimes, we might even realize this as the moment happens, which can create a profound sense of loss or sadness as the moment wanes and eventually passes completely.

Think of marvel or wonder as the emotional equivalent of adrenaline. It's a short burst of powerful, intense emotional energy that drastically changes our experience of that moment. As a result, this type of savoring is crazy effective at stopping or slowing down time and helps place our problems in a more positive perspective. A particularly great example of how marveling impacts someone's perception of time took place high above the planet. A NASA mission specialist, Laurel Clark, described seeing a sunset in space as one of the most incredible moments of her entire fucking life: "There's a flash; the whole payload bay turns this rosy pink. It only lasts about 15 seconds and then it's gone. It's very ethereal and extremely beautiful." For an experienced astronaut to describe a 15-second period of time as the most memorable moment of her career? That really fucking says something. Hell, it makes me want to go to space even more than I did as a kid!

## Why Should We Care?

My memory frequently drifts back (and reminisces) on a specific summer night of my misspent teenaged youth in 1991, and it does this for no apparently discernible reason. In the middle of an area of my city affectionately known as "Felony Flats," there I was with three of my friends, sitting around a beat-up old picnic table in my friend's backyard, which was completely devoid of vegetation but rich in dust and rocks.

We began our conversation sometime after sunset, most likely discussing Michael Jordan's domination over the rest of the world, before moving on to girls, cars, and other subjects critically important to 16-year-old boys. We trash-talked one another, experimented with creative ways to curse, made crude jokes out of one another's vocal missteps, and lived our lives in that beautiful fucking moment without a single care in the world. There was nothing remarkable about that conversation, but it effortlessly slid into the late hours of the night and into the early morning.

We didn't find a cure for cancer or the secret to world peace. Not one of us formulated the unifying theory of everything. Hell, I couldn't tell you the precise date to save my life. Every last fucking time I tell this story and recall this memory with great fondness, no more than a second passes before someone else recalls a highly similar story. Shit, I bet you're thinking of your own at this moment. Why in the fresh red hell is this story so relatable, and why does it seem so clear in my memory, as well as everyone else's memories of their own?

It's easy to see that relationships and dialogue are a large part of the reason, as most similar stories share those elements predictably. The most telling aspect of the story is rooted in the idea of mindful presence. None of us were distracted. Nobody was checking their fucking phones, since ours were still mounted to the walls inside the house back then. There were no notifications to interrupt us, no cameras to record and snap every last fucking moment, no memes to share, and whenever our conversations reached a lull, nobody checked out to go play some mindless game; we persisted and used boredom as our impetus to take the conversation in a totally new direction until we were fully tapped out, which was sometime before the sun came up.

Mihaly Csikszentmihalyi, permanent champion of the least-likely-to-be-spelled-or-pronounced-correctly name of all time (I bet the poor guy probably never found a keychain with his name on it), theorized that situations like this represent a state of "flow" or interactions marked by a general lack of restrictions and an effortless push-pull relationship, where participants in the interaction play seamlessly off of one another. Without distractions disrupting this sense of flow, it disrupts participants' perceptions of time. This partially explains why, when we find ourselves in such a state, time flies away, and before we know what happened, we've clocked eight hours on the phone with a loved one. This usually takes place among family members who haven't talked for a while or with lovers during that super special, yet fleeting honeymoon phase of the relationship.

This state of flow was not unique to the early 90s. The mere existence of pervasive forms of technology and media entities vying for our attention at every hour of each day does not preclude us from pursuit of flow. It merely takes a conscious, intentional, deliberate, and relentless desire to reclaim control over our time and attention, and of course, to put the fucking phone down.

### Chapter Challenge: Sava the Flava

This one is fun — like really fucking fun and memorable — so I hope you enjoy it as much as I do. It's a GREAT activity to do with children, but you can choose anyone important to your life to do it with, so that's the first step. Pick someone to enjoy a meal with, but as with before, it's not going to be any old meal. Ideally, this is a person you care about and someone with whom you want to improve or deepen your relationship.

Set aside dedicated time for this one. You'll probably want to set aside an entire evening. Second, when the person comes over or is available to kick things off, take away that person's phone. Shut it down. Yes, power it the fuck off. Yours, too. Put them away, somewhere out of sight and out of arm's reach. Then, make sure you do the same with any computers, tablets, and yes, even the television. The idea here is to go 100% screen-free. A bit of music is okay, but if you must play it from your phone over a Bluetooth speaker like our family does, ensure the phone is well out of reach and sight.

Next, start cooking — together! Working in concert with the other person, prepare your meal from scratch as a team. It doesn't matter if you know what the fuck you're doing or not. This ain't the fucking Food Network Challenge or Master Chef, and Gordon Ramsey isn't going to show up at your house to make fun of your overcooked scallops. Pick a meal to make and go for it. If you imbibe, bring some good wine or beer into the picture. Enjoy yourselves. Laugh. Converse!

As the evening unfolds, concentrate on savoring every last fucking moment together. Listen to the other person as though this might be the last conversation you ever have together (without making it weird and melodramatic, of course). As the conversation develops and settles into a state of flow, ride that fucking wave like a professional surfer and don't stop. Don't overthink it, either, because too much thought quickly kills the flow. Simply let go, immerse yourself in that moment, and focus on enjoying the interaction for whatever it may be. Bonus points if, afterward, you do the dishes together as well. Sometimes, that's even more fun than the dinner, especially if it turns into an all-out water fight in the kitchen.

Don't be surprised if this evening goes long. I've frequently heard stories from my students that these dinners lasted until 2 or 3 in the morning without realizing where the time went. On the other hand, if it doesn't have that super flowy feel to it, spend some time thinking about why. What distracted you, the other person, or both of you? What disrupted or restricted the flow? Try to learn from this if the conditions weren't perfect, and don't be afraid to try it again. Don't let your expectations sour you on the whole experience. Remember, like a gardener, you can only create the conditions for savoring to happen. At some point, it's up to the seed.

Perhaps the next day, spend some more time thinking about what, if anything, gave this evening a different 'feel' than others in the past. How did the act of intentional, mindful presence play a part in tilling the soil and making it fertile enough for savoring and flow to take place? What might happen if you pursued evenings like this more frequently? What's stopping you from doing so?

# 9

## *THE PURSUIT OF ~~ANXIETY AND REGRET~~ HAPPINESS*

In the last chapter, we discovered more about savoring and what happens when we actually put the fucking phone down and learn to live a little. That's great and all, but we've been talking a lot about the concept of mindfulness in this book as well, so it's time we combined the two concepts to see how one promotes the other. The iconic Ferris Bueller once mused: "Life moves pretty fast. If you don't stop to look around once in a while, you might miss it." A-fucking-men, Mr. Bueller, and well said. If I were to update that at all for the modern age, I might say something like, oh, I don't know: Put the fucking phone down, because life can't wait. Sound familiar? Of course, it does, for fuck's sake, it's on the cover and in the running header on every other page. When we get to the intersection of mindful presence and savoring, we'll find happiness on the corner waiting for us. Once there, we'll kick anxiety and regret's asses to the curb, so let's take a drive down there now.

According to research into savoring done by Fred Bryant out of Loyola University Chicago and Joseph Veroff from University of Michigan, we can enhance the shit out of our savoring experiences in five different ways, all of which connect directly to everything we've learned so far about becoming more mindfully present:

- Absorbing the moment: When we fully allow ourselves to surrender to the moment while savoring, we open up more possibilities for savoring to take place.
- Sharpening the senses: As we continue developing the ability to become mindful and bring ourselves into awareness of each of our

senses, we can use such intention to more sharply focus on the sensations of the moment—both physical and emotional.

- Memory-building: When we capture a piece of a moment and associate it with something tangible, like a picture, trinket, or souvenir, we provide ourselves with a physical means to reminisce on the moment later.
- Sharing: Either by physically sharing a savored moment with other people (preferred) or by sharing the moment via communication (i.e., telling a friend about the experience), we engage in what George Herbert Mead called *symbolic interaction*, which helps us make sense out of the experience, further cementing the moment into the recesses of our memories.
- Self-congratulation: Specifically, this method relates to the basking type of savoring, when we reminisce on the steps or difficulties leading up to a win, and then this enhances the feeling of victory at the moment of basking. For example, if an author worked for years to finish a book, then the moment the box of print copies shows up, that provides an opportunity to reflect on the journey it took to arrive at that moment.

## At the Intersection of Mindfulness and Savoring

Obviously, for us to practice all these elements of savoring, we have to be doing anything but staring at our fucking phones. We have to be present, centered in the moment, and we have to do so on purpose, with deliberate intention. What's fascinating about the relationship between mindfulness and savoring is that one enhances the other through a symbiotic relationship. The more potential for savoring the moment, the more it pulls us into the present, but conversely, the more present we are, the more likely we will find something to savor about that moment.

If you have a much better memory than mine (remember the grocery store story about the four items all starting with the letter P?), then you will recall that mindfulness is made up of four components: present-centered awareness, intention, the ability to notice changes in the moment, and nonjudgmental acceptance. While present-centered awareness may seem like a pretty fucking obvious prerequisite to savoring, how do the other three components affect this process?

### *Intention*

It's totally possible to savor a moment without being mindfully immersed in the moment on purpose. A summertime thunderstorm out my slider door, a magnificent sunset, the view from Palouse Falls in Washington State (seriously, Google that shit sometime) — are all grand examples of marvel or awe-inducing sights that don't require me to make a choice to be present, partly because their grandiosity does the job for me.

Making the conscious choice to put the fucking phone down and be present in the moment, without distraction, however, most definitely increases the potential for additional savoring to take place. Like Mr. Bueller said, stop and take a look around once in a while or we might miss life as it happens. The key is the first step: just fucking stop. We have to make a concerted effort to do so, and part of that comes with the territory when we set aside screen-free time on a regular basis. By doing so, we return control to ourselves over our attention, which makes us much more likely to make such a choice later.

### *The Discovery of Novelty*

Sure, we can be immersed in the moment on purpose, but if we aren't prepared to discover the newness or what changes take place during each moment, then we aren't all that likely to savor anything, so the discovery of novelty is pretty goddamn important to this process. Otherwise, we're spacing out. Granted, there's something to be said for a great space-out, but if we want to really fucking appreciate and savor more of our moments, we'd better prepare ourselves to discern what's cool about any given moment.

There's a great poem by T.S. Eliot, in which is a line that provides endless inspiration for me: "We shall not cease from exploration, and the end of all our exploring will be to arrive where we started and know the place for the first time." Seeing something again for the first time may sound like a contradiction in terms, but it involves seeing something mundane through more imaginative, creative eyes. Think about it. Children are fucking geniuses at this. To a child, everything is new and full of potential, but somewhere along the way, we told our creative lenses to fuck off, and we started viewing the world through dulled, jaded eyes. To become mindful is to see things with that creative spirit once again and develop a whole new appreciation for the power of the moment.

### *Nonjudgmental Acceptance*

We probably all know someone who fails to appreciate the beauty and grace of simply shutting the fuck up and enjoying their lives. These people are likely cursed with the characteristic of bitterness, which, by the way, is a trait recently added to the Diagnostic and Statistical Manual of Disorders that psychiatrists use to diagnose mental illness. Such people are miserable fucking assholes who suck the life out of every last experience, which is why we tend to avoid them, but let's ponder why they seem to be incapable of savoring. They fucking judge every goddamned experience of their natural lives, rendering themselves completely incapable of joy.

Now, let's ponder who might be the polar opposite of such a miserable succubus. Before I started teaching, I worked as a human resources executive for a large red-and-khaki wearing national retail corporation. I won't say which one, but you can probably surmise it. Part of my job entailed travel to various stores in our district to perform store inspections. At one store, there was this custodial supervisor who came in every night around closing time, and he was always sickeningly upbeat. In fact, he was so annoyingly positive that I couldn't help but contract his attitude like a fucking virus. It was like he had some strange gravitational field surrounding him that drew others closer to his vicinity, if only to pick up some positivity through osmosis. One night, out of burning curiosity (a side effect of catching the positivity virus), I asked him why he was always so happy. He laughed his contagious chortle and responded:

*Josh, every single day you see me is the best day of my life, and I'll tell you why. If I have managed to wake up again, greeted by the potential for another day in which to get things right, then I have awoken to the greatest day of my life.*

My jaw dropped to the fucking floor when I heard that, rendering me speechless, which is no easy feat.

Later, as I reflected on what he said, I realized the truth in what he was talking about, as well as how his view is related to mindfulness. The reason he was so ready and able to savor the experiences of his life, no matter how seemingly shitty his job may have been (I've done custodial work, so my hat goes off to those capable of bearing what us lazy fuckers cannot), was because he was intentionally and consciously centered in the moment, curious and open to new things, and he took things as they came without suffering kneejerk reactions and judging those experiences like an asshole. As a result, this dude was not only remarkably positive and upbeat, which, drew others into his orbit, but he also had the patience of a fucking saint and the innovative creativity of a goddamn genius. By the way, these qualities seem to be additional side effects of mindfulness, and they're just beginning to be researched across the globe.

## Mindfulness + Savoring + Interaction

Being mindful isn't a guarantee of savoring. Rather, like I mentioned earlier, it's like being a gardener. A good gardener knows to till the soil, pull weeds and rocks, fertilize, and water the soil after planting a seed. In other words, the gardener uses care to create the conditions necessary for something to grow and then waits patiently. As the plant grows, the gardener continues nourishing the plant until whatever the fuck he planted does what it's supposed to do (bloom, fruit, flower, carpet the fucking yard with leaves each autumn, etc.). As with this metaphor, we simply create the conditions for savoring to take place by centering ourselves in the moment, on purpose and with intention; we discern the novelty of the moment; and we accept things as they happen. This way, we notice when the time is ripe to savor, as well as how to prolong the enjoyment of that moment as needed.

## Story Time!

One of the most memorable interactions demonstrating this relationship occurred between Stacie (my partner) and I in 2012. It was a weekend, and we were trapped inside because of the stupid fucking Pacific Northwest rain that never fucking ends, especially in the spring. Guess what time of year I'm writing this chapter? As a result, we were going bat-shit crazy, and that meant emotions were running hot. Stacie started yelling at the kids a bit excessively, even considering the irritably rainy day. We were cleaning the house, but the more Stacie cleaned, the more irritable she became (mostly because of all the shit she kept finding under the couch), and the yelling not only became more frequent, but it also started getting darker and more personal. This wasn't your typical I'm-in-a-bad-fucking-mood-so-don't-fuck-with-me moments.

I started worrying when I saw my kids' faces and their obvious display of butthurt, but they stayed quiet (a very wise choice) and continued cleaning. Summoning all my infinite idiocy, I suggested maybe she should take it down a notch. That, obviously, was TNT on a fucking inferno. Predictably, I became the target of her rage, and on any other day, I would have snapped back, and we would have bickered for a good two or more hours, but there was something about this situation that struck me. I was intentionally present and noticed there was something different about this time – something *novel.*

I walked up to her, took her hand, which she snapped away, growling, "Don't fucking touch me!" I sat down on the couch and calmly asked her to sit with me. "Fuck you, I don't want to," she snapped. I persisted, imploring her as calmly as possible to take a time-out. She slumped into the couch, "Fine."

I put my hand on her knee cautiously, half expecting a set of teeth to open up at her kneecap and amputate my hand whole, but then I asked, "What's wrong?"

"Why does something have to be wrong," she fired back, "Can't you just let me have a bad day?"

"Normally, yes. . ." I continued, "but not today. This is different." I became even more mindful of my tone, ensuring that what I said next expressed sincere concern and without even a microgram of snark, "*Something* is wrong, and I want you to talk to me. I'm worried about you."

At that, she paused, and it was like I saw her anger and rage melt away, leaving behind a vulnerable, pained expression, dressed up with the tears streaming down her face. My wife, by the way is not a crier. She calls me a little bitch all the time for the fact that I cry way too easily, as though my tear duct and urinary tract were switched at birth. Her tears gave way to sobs, and I put my arm around her, pulling her closer and placing her head on my chest.

As she sobbed, she lamented her grandmother, who was, at the time, being moved from advanced care to hospice, knowing that the end of her life was imminent. Her grandmother was a saint who acted as the matriarch of my wife's gargantuan Viking family, not to mention one of the kindest, gentlest, most compassionate humans I have ever had the honor and pleasure of knowing. As my wife's façade unraveled, I recognized the need to be even more mindful than usual, because it was my presence and the gift of listening that was affording her the opportunity to open up and unload.

Her rage prior to this interaction was merely a *symptom*, as anger almost always is. Anger is a secondary emotion—a mask we wear when we are unable to productively and healthily cope with difficult emotions—in her case, grief and worry. Without being mindful enough to recognize her anger as a symptom and not a sign of lashing out at me personally, not only would I have fanned the flames and exasperated an already painful situation by unnecessarily fighting over something so insanely fucking insignificant, but I would have failed to help the woman I love work through her emotions and cope with an incredibly goddamned difficult time in her life.

Once she finished articulating her worry, with me listening mindfully (giving her the necessary space to open up without judgment or attempting to "fix" her), all the anger dissipated. She thanked me for listening and then apologized to our children, explaining the grave nature of the situation to each of them. Through mindful presence, I not only helped her work her way through anger, grief, and worry, but I helped her become more mindful and calm as well, which she then demonstrated in her request for forgiveness from our children. Even more to the point, she was able to be mindfully present for our kids, as she broke the news of her grandmother to them. I like to use the metaphor of a tree in a windstorm to explore situations like this: Once the wind dies down, the branches will thank the trunk for its stability. That's some Zen shit right there.

Throughout our interaction, I found myself experiencing the thanksgiving form of savoring, as the lesson of mindful presence was a gift I had learned elsewhere and was exceedingly grateful to have used in such a generative way. Any other day, I would have blindly duked it out with my wife over something stupid, but the moral of this tale is to consciously watch for situations in which mindfulness is the best choice of action.

If we want to learn to stop chasing anxiety and regret and instead pursue happiness, as this chapter's title implies, we have to learn to put the fucking phone down and take a bit of time off once in a while.

### Chapter Challenge: Everyday Vacations

The following challenge is something that should take at least a week, so even if you want to finish this book and move on with your life, you should really break for a week and see how this goes. After that, pick up where you left off, but understand that this one's results take a little while to experience.

The first step is to plan for and complete a 20-minute "vacation" from your everyday routine each and every day. This vacation should be spent doing something fun and enjoyable, but the only major rule is, you probably guessed it, NO SCREENS. If the weather is nice, go for a walk, run, hike, or even spend some time outside gardening. Go out for coffee or ice cream, visit an art gallery, take an extra-long bath, spend time with a good friend, or combine any of these together. Go to an art gallery with a friend while simultaneously eating ice cream and bathing. On second thought, don't do that.

Each day, before your vacation, jot down your worries, stresses, or anxieties at that moment. Consider it a sort of "worry log" where you can write these down and temporarily store them while you're checked out of normal life for 20 minutes. Don't spend too much time writing them down; quick summaries will be fine. Also, don't invent new worries as a result. Stick to only your concerns of the moment.

While on vacation, take the time to purposefully attend to any and all aspects of that give you joy. Notice the joy as it arises and from what source it springs. As you absorb and savor that feeling, swish it around in your mind like you might savor a fine wine.

Once your vacation for the day is over, the next thing you should immediately do is plan the vacation for the next day. Decide what you want to do, have a backup plan in case the weather changes, and put the vacation in your phone as a reminder, with an alarm.

At the end of the day, as you lay down to go to sleep, spend a bit of time thinking back to your vacation for that day. Revisit it in as much detail as possible and allow yourself to reminisce on the elation it provided. Let that memory be the last thing you think about before drifting off.

The next day, repeat this process. Then, at the end of 7 full days of vacations, take time to reflect back on each of the vacations you took over the last week. Try to identify what gave you the greatest bang for your buck each day, as well as which day was your favorite. Then, compare how you feel at the end of the week with how you felt when you started.

Were you happier at the end of the week? If you're like the thousands of others who have tried this experiment, then odds are, you're a hell of a lot happier.

How did writing down your worries and concerns impact the way you experienced your vacations? This practice is like extracting concerns for us, and once they're on the page, it allows us to bookmark them for later so they don't occupy our every waking thought. Also, once we come back to those worries with a fresh set of eyes, we often find that our anxieties and concerns weren't quite as bad as we initially thought. There's something about seeing our anxieties take on a physical form on a page. They don't seem as shitty that way.

How did paying attention to your happiness as it arose affect you? Did it help to prolong the enjoyment of the activity?

How did the planning process affect you? This part of the activity exercises our ability to anticipate and savor moments that haven't yet happened. After doing this for a while, we begin to look forward to the future, and when we give ourselves something to look forward to, especially when it doesn't involve staring into a tiny fucking screen, we continue to develop our ability to anticipate, thereby generating a higher degree of happiness and fulfillment.

How did reminiscing each night and at the end of the week affect your happiness? When we revisit our happiest memories, we consciously shift focus, much like the custodial supervisor whose story I mentioned earlier. By training ourselves to shift away from the negative and look more at the positive, we bump out the shittier parts of life and learn to focus more on what actually makes life worth living.

# 10

# CHANGING EXPECTATIONS TO APPRECIATE WHAT WE HAVE

We've all heard the corny-as-shit water glass analogy to describe one's orientation toward life. The optimist, typically annoying as fuck, claims the glass is half-full. The pessimist, typically depressing as fuck, bitches and complains that the glass is half-empty. The dorky-ass realist steps in to make a cheesy joke about the ratio of air to water being precisely equal, and nobody else gets the joke because it goes right over their heads. Meanwhile, I'm the opportunist who drank the goddamn water while everyone else was paralyzed by inaction. Better luck next time, assholes.

We've also seen a shit-ton of inspirational kitten posters or images of unnaturally pretty scenery plastered with quotes about how life is all perception or some other bullshit designed to distract us from the fact that we're all exploited and underpaid for our efforts. I won't sit here and blow smoke up anyone's poopchute by suggesting somehow that changing perceptions is the secret key to happiness or whatever. Instead, I'll fucking tell you *how* to go about making such a change, or at least a goddamn good start in the right direction.

In the field of communication, an amazingly brilliant woman named Judee Burgoon, who also never found a keychain with her name on it her entire life, came up with a seriously brilliant theory: Expectancy Violation Theory. This idea suggests that our interactions with one another are all based on an unspoken and unwritten series of expectations. When those expectations are violated, it results in a predictable reaction, either positively or negatively charged, but never neutral. For example, if I go out to my mailbox, and there's a check from the government for $10,000 because I overpaid taxes or something else that would only happen in a deranged fever dream, my reaction would be overwhelmingly positive, as I scream like a girl at a K-pop concert. On the other hand, if I opened a letter from the government with a bill for $10,000 because I didn't pay enough, which is the more believable scenario, then my reaction would be negative, and I'd stomp my feet like a toddler at Walmart who didn't get the toy he wanted. Our expectations shape how we make sense out of our interactions with one another and the world in general. As soon as we accept that, we can shape the outcome of a situation by consciously reshaping our expectations.

One of my favorite parenting mantras is, "To the child with a hammer, everything looks like a nail." Ain't that the fucking truth? If you don't believe me, give literally any fucking kid a hammer and see how long it takes before you need an insurance claim. A child, deprived of any other entertainment, will actively seek out new and unusual means to use a hammer other than its intended purpose, and we (alleged) adults are no different. When someone is predisposed to bitterness, everything in their orbit looks like potential for complaints, and this is because such a person walks through life expecting to be disappointed. Naturally, such a person is easily able to find that disappointment anywhere and everywhere. To a cynic, even a sequel to the greatest fucking sci-fi saga of all time, a movie fanboys and girls alike have waited several generations to receive, becomes the object of their ire. Fucking fanboys; this is why we can't have nice things.

If our proverbial pessimist trots around with a metaphorical hammer made from the make-believe Criticisium alloy, seeking out things to destroy for themselves and others alike, then how can the rest who are not infected with bitterness make conscious and intentional decisions to avoid such behavior? My solution is super fun to say, and we covered it way back in Chapter 3: perturbation. Remember, to perturb a situation is to knock some element of it off-course by causing a systematic deviation that changes everything about the outcome of a situation. It's the wrench in the fucking machine that shatters the rest.

Behavior, much like objects in physics, has momentum. The stronger the momentum (replace mass in this equation with the length of time one has been repeating the behavior), the harder the force required to perturb the system. If someone has been a little bitch about something for more than 20 years, then it's highly unlikely that person can read a kickass book like this one and wake up the next morning ready to change. A perturbation to a system like that is going to take some serious fucking muscle, and to build it requires a serious fucking workout, which I'll explain later, after yet another story break.

### Story Time!

Back when I was a doctoral student, I spent several classes next to a Filipino Catholic priest named Jim, who I'm pretty sure called himself that because his actual name was far too hard for Americans to get right.

Fucking Americans. He was a quiet guy who rarely spoke up in class, and I think most of us simply assumed that, because he was an ESL student, he was too nervous, self-conscious, or shy to speak up. That was before we all got to know him and what a wise fucking dude he was. Jim wasn't quiet because he had to be; Jim was quiet because he deliberately chose to be silent. Jim was listening, and while he took everything in, he methodically shaped and distilled his contribution to our discussions until they were of the highest possible quality. In a 16-week class, I heard Jim speak up in class discussions three or four times, so whenever he spoke, everyone would listen because we knew that shit was pure gold.

One day, we had a class discussion on cultivating gratitude, and our group's conversation was absolutely electric. The discussion moved so effortlessly that we could barely get our thoughts out before the conversation took another detour. Predictably, everyone but Jim contributed. Our professor noticed, so he invited Jim to speak, and when that happened, I'll never forget the look on Jim's face. He seemed so genuinely pleased to have someone notice him and ask his opinion, but he didn't answer immediately. Instead, he leaned back in his desk, and after a cat-like stretch that felt like an eternity, Jim took a deep breath and subsequent pause before he began. The suspense was simultaneously fucking awful and beautiful. He then opened his mouth and said one of the most profound things I have ever heard, to this day:

> *How odd is it that we don't appreciate our health until we are sick? And how odd is it that we do not take notice of the very breath that keeps us alive until running up a flight of stairs threatens to take it from us? Oh, the good it would do us to learn to appreciate the many miracles of life before they are gone!*

Jim was abso-fucking-lutely right. As I left class, I remember walking aimlessly outside for a while before driving home, suddenly noticing the crisp, spring air. The colors all around me seemed more intense and vivid, and the long freeway drive back home took a little longer, partly because I didn't feel rushed. Jim's comment was my perturbance, snapping me out of a rut of thinking and behaving, causing me to suddenly notice more. His comment made me look at the Criticismium hammer in my own hand, and that was the day I decided to drop it in favor of gratitude.

Ready to put the fucking phone down and give this workout a shot?

### Chapter Challenge: Cultivating Gratitude

Each and every single day of your life for the next six weeks, write down five things you are grateful for at that moment, and do this at the beginning of your day. If you wake up at six o'clock in the morning, then I'm incredibly sorry for you because I hate mornings, but do it anyway. If you're a late sleeper and don't get up until noon, rest assured that I, along with all other parents in the world, hate your fucking guts, but do it then. If you work graveyard shift and don't get up until afternoon, then goddamn, you are a strong motherfucker, but do it then. The point of this exercise is to *start* your day with five things for which to be grateful, so set an extra alarm as a reminder if necessary. It is absolutely fucking critical that you stick to this schedule and not miss a day. Date each set of five items so you can look back on them later, but here's the real challenge: You can't repeat any one item during this six-week period.

Look, this challenge is tough as fuck, but it's not impossible, so don't be a little bitch about it like I was the first time I approached it. Odds are, you'll start out with cheesy, generic shit like: "I'm so grateful for 1) sunshine, 2) my dog, 3) my spouse, 4) coffee, and 5) my bed. Super!" Don't feel bad if this is literally your first day (it only means you're basic — for now). The trick to this list, and part of what makes it such an interesting challenge, is that, later on, you'll dig deeper and make your list more specific, like "I'm grateful for 1) the feeling of the sun on my back, 2) the way my dog greets me when she first sees me, 3) a healthy marriage, 4) the smell of fresh coffee brewing, and 5) a great night's sleep, thanks to my bed." This doesn't make you any less basic for being grateful for these items, but it does force you to be more specific with where you distribute your gratitude.

Look, this gratitude list doesn't need to sound like Ralph Waldo Emerson. If you want to be grateful for a fucking stapler because you need to join paper together, then so be it. Relish that red fucking Swingline before your boss snags it from you and asks you to move your desk for the umpteenth time. I've expressed my gratitude for office supplies before. There's no shame. Your gratitude is your gratitude, so who the fuck would dare to take that away from you? Own that shit like a boss.

As one might easily predict, you'll run out of basic ideas as this challenge progresses, and you'll have to dig much deeper for things to be grateful for. At the end of six weeks, you'll have a list that inspires greater joy than any-fucking-thing Marie Kondo could ever conjure. Seriously, you'll have somewhere over 200 items on your list that bring you serious fucking joy and remind you what makes life worth living. That is something to celebrate.

If you miss a day or forget, that's fine. It's like taking antibiotics, where if you miss a dose, double up when you can, and get your ass back on track. That's an interesting metaphor, isn't it? A gratitude list is like an antibiotic for life, and much like starting a Z-pack, you'll notice yourself feeling better in a matter of days.

Of course, this won't make you shit rainbows, and if it does, it's probably not because of the challenge. See a doctor. There will be times in the challenge where your list dips into darkness. As we awaken and strengthen gratitude muscles, we tend to compare our new grateful perspective with our older, outdated ways of taking things for granted, and when this happens, it can easily kick up feelings of guilt or remorse. The best thing to do in such a case would be to exercise the mindfulness characteristic of nonjudgmental acceptance: acknowledge the feeling, and allow it to pass without latching onto it.

The real key to success in this challenge is not quality or poetic essence of your list, but rather, in consistency of writing each and every day as you start your day. Don't judge your goddamn choices of gratitude! Go with the flow, and you'll develop a keen eye for gratitude as the experiment continues. It may not seem like something as simple as writing down five things each day at the start of every day would make a tremendous fucking impact on your life, but over time, what this practice does is shift our perspective and transform our expectations, which has an abso-fucking-lutely seismic impact. Over the course of six weeks, here's what you can expect to happen:

For the first week, you're simply trying to get yourself into the habit. Expect your list to be shallow, predictable, and dull. Persist with that shit anyway.

In the second week, your habits are solidifying, and you may even find yourself "collecting" items and experiences to write down the next day. For example, after I've already written down my five items to start my day, I might find something totally new to be grateful for and bookmark that in my mind for the next morning. This isn't cheating; it's simply playing smart.

By the third week, the list has been engrained into your routine, and you might even feel a little anticipation for the moment you wake up and start jotting things down. You'll probably start collecting things more frequently to the point where you have more than five items each day, forcing you to narrow them down to the top five. Think about that — having *too many* things to be grateful for each morning. . .

In the fourth week, you're refining how you articulate your gratitude items, and you'll start discerning the difference between actual gratitude and what I call 'backhanded' gratitude. For example, backhanded gratitude may sound like, "I am so fucking glad my bitch-monster of an ex is no longer a part of my life." Seriously? Is that gratitude or an opportunity for you to bitch about someone who can't respond? Concentrate on the positive and avoid implying insults or complaints by wrapping it up in fancy words iced over with gratitude.

By weeks five and six, you'll start noticing real, tangible, and radical transformation. I'm not going to spoil it for you, but trust me when I say that doing this challenge regularly, each and every day, will cause a complete and utter shift to your perceptions. As each day unfolds, you will see things differently, and suddenly, you find yourself focusing much more on the positive and much less on the negative. It builds resilience, as well as an attitude of gratitude, which is more than merely a cheesy AF rhyme — it's actually a scientific concept. The space in your mind formerly leased by a Criticismium hammer is freed up for new renters, allowing gratitude to move into the empty spot. Instead of searching for things to criticize, you become a collector of all that is good, and trust me when I state that the good weighs significantly less than the shitty stuff.

Gratitude opens up the potential to the abundance of life all around us. As our attention turns away from our fucking phones and onto that for which we are grateful, we'll find the source for that gratitude, illuminating the complicated web of interconnection all around us, which is such a mind-blowing sensation. Gratitude forces us to recognize all the good that comes in from all around us, which, in turn, motivates and inspires us to do good for others and resolve to continue doing so in the future. Gratitude perturbs us, which creates and sustains optimism through derailing negative thought patterns.

Gratitude, once developed, is a motherfucking game-changer, but it is one that absolutely must be felt and experienced to be understood, so it does you no good to merely read my take on it. Get the fuck out of here and start living your own gratefulness.

You sure as shit won't regret it.

# 11

## GUERRILLA GRATITUDE

Before we kick this off, you're still doing the gratitude list every day, right? If not, then this chapter might not make a lot of sense. Even if you have done some sort of daily gratitude practice before, try it the way I suggested. Hell, even if you've done it the way I proposed, do it again. It's critically important for us to be on the same page, in the same ballpark, and a whole bunch of other stupid togetherness metaphors for shit like that. Gratitude has to be primed and pumped before we move any further, and the point of this gratitude practice is to shift our perception through deliberate intention, because in this chapter, we're going to take that sensation of gratitude and intensify that bitch like a mofo.

We all know by now that gratitude is feeling grateful for having received something from some external entity. It's not hard to feel super grateful for a bit of sunshine and temperatures that steadily stay above freezing, especially in mid-March in the Pacific Northwest. The winter in which I've been writing this book (2018-19) has been the longest fucking winter of my life, and I've been living here for 40 years. My front yard in mid-March has at least two feet of snow, and considering my distaste for frozen white death powder, that means I'm feeling really fucking grateful to see all that snow die the slow melt-demise it deserves.

When I feel this gratitude, it produces a noticeable uptick to my mood, but a really fascinating thing happens when I *share* my snowicidal thoughts with others in my area. They laugh, nod rapidly, and commiserate on the painful extent of this winter and all the associated inconvenience it brought to our little corner of the world. Suddenly, we're sharing a moment of happiness, at which point, I realize that my happiness doubled through sharing. Unlike currency, time, or any fucking other commodity, when we share happiness, we don't need to divvy it up into smaller pieces, because, as we share happiness, it magically doubles. Too bad that doesn't happen with anything else, amirite?

It is precisely this act of sharing happiness that we are going to focus on for this chapter, through the practice of sharing gratitude through the expression of appreciation. We'll also take a look at the prerequisites to do so effectively so that we can maximize our chances for this mysterious doubling of good will.

### Target-ed Gratitude

Whenever I talk about the power behind the expression of appreciation, I love to share a story of when it really hit me regarding how much power appreciation can have. Remember way back in Chapter 9 when I mentioned that I was once a miserable human resources executive for an unnamed red-and-khaki-wearing retail corporation? One of my primary responsibilities as an HR exec was to keep employees (who we were always instructed to refer to as *team members*, as if somehow a retail employee by any other name isn't miserable working Black Friday) satisfied. I won't say *happy* here, because it takes a seriously special or deranged person to be happy in retail; for the most part, everyone there accepts the misery of their fate. One of the challenges of my position was to mediate damage from employees, I mean *team members*, whose misery spilled over onto others, because negativity is seriously like a fast-spreading virus in most organizations, but in retail, that virus may as well be the Black Death.

I had been studying gratitude as I pursued my master's degree in communication while working for this unnamed (but super easy to guess) retail giant, and I wanted to play a little game by conducting an experiment in the power of gratitude. I went to my boss and asked permission for the experiment I'm about to explain, at which point, he laughed hysterically and suggested my "liberal, hippie, touchy-feely bullshit" was going to backfire. Not one to miss out on an opportunity to see me fail miserably, he agreed.

The next morning, at our daily all-employee (goddammit, I mean *team member*) meeting before opening the store, my boss and I gathered everyone together and arranged the 40 or so of us in a kumbaya-style circle, at which point everyone assumed it was either group therapy or story time. We then initiated my experiment by announcing we were going to go around the circle, where everyone was going to verbally say thank-you to someone else in the circle for any reason they could think of, until everyone had a chance to express appreciation for someone else. As my boss predicted, I saw a few eyes roll so hard that I thought it might force the person into a backward somersault. Still, my boss kicked things off by pointing to one of the people across from him and thanking that person for doing a great job of keeping the bathroom clean. Funny thing was, that person was one of the people who rolled their eyes at the commencement of the activity, and yet, here she was, blushing and grinning from one ear to the fucking other.

Initially, the thank-yous were cheesy as fuck, but then a funny thing happened, as they became increasingly sincere. About halfway around the circle, the gratitude became more meaningful, and I could even see a few of the recipients of that appreciation wiping at their eyes. Stiff posture and blatant lack of motivation (because, seriously, who really likes working early fucking mornings in retail, anyway?) started loosening up. Hands animated, laughter grew louder, and even the seemingly impenetrable tough-guy façade of some of the brawniest backroom dudes cracked under the weight of all that juicy liberal hippie bullshit. It was a Tuesday morning, and by five o'clock when I left that evening, there was a palpable change in attitude that hung heavy in the air, overpowering even the stench of popcorn at the front of the store.

I stopped by my boss' office before I left and peeked in the door, smiling. "Wanna do it again tomorrow?" I asked, assuring that I showed him my best I-fucking-told-you-so-you-arrogant-asshole grin. He rolled his eyes, reminiscent of the team member from earlier that day, "Yeah, why not?"

The daily thank-you circle took no time at all to become a permanent fixture of that store's weekly routine. Suddenly, people went out of their way to help others in the hopes they might end up somebody's mention during the next team huddle. I never before saw such a radical overnight transformation in behavior, especially in fucking retail! Eventually, it grew to the point where we threw ourselves into yet another new program, this time one where team members could thank one another using a cheap-to-print business cards tacked to a bulletin board in the breakroom. Once a month, we held a drawing for some amazing prize, like Bose headphones or a brand-new, whole iPod (as opposed to just a piece of one). Even our company metrics started reporting differently, as employee (fuck, *team member*) complaints declined, turnover nearly went non-existent for a brief period, and our team satisfaction scores fucking soared, which later benefitted me in a tangible manner, as these scores were tied to my yearly bonus structure. Believe me, when I got that check, I felt extra motherfucking grateful! Interestingly enough, my boss got a higher check as well, and trust me – he wasn't calling it liberal hippie bullshit anymore. I had a convert on my hands.

There is a dark side to the expression of appreciation, though. It's not all bonus checks, unicorns, rainbows, and other hippie bullshit. For us to express appreciation activates a sense of vulnerability. After all, if I go off and tell my wife I'm grateful that she doesn't put up with my arrogant ass and calls me out on my bullshit, then for a brief moment, I'm uplifting her to a point of reverence, which means that, relatively speaking, I have to lower myself. In doing so, she has momentary power over me, and if she reacts by pulling some shit like, "Yeah, and don't you fucking forget it, little man," then that further relegates me to my tiny corner place and increases the power gap between the two of us. Fortunately, she doesn't react like that, and honestly, few of us ever would when being thanked, but that's not how our gut instincts see things, is it? Our guts are always telling us that this scenario is as likely as any other, so we have a tendency to feel a bit of humbling vulnerability when confronting the unknown like this.

By the way, there's a massive fucking chasm of difference between the concepts of humility and humiliation. The two words may share the same basic root and sound similar, but each one has a vastly different focal point. When we feel humiliated, we feel shame. As Brenè Brown stated the difference between guilt and shame, guilt is when we feel like we've failed at something, while shame is when we feel like we *are* the fucking failure. Humiliation is the kind of embarrassment that makes us want to run away, hide, and never be seen or heard from again. With feeling humiliation, the focus is primarily on ourselves. Humility, on the other hand, is what we feel when we uplift others to a higher position than ourselves. The focal point for this feeling is *always* on the betterment of others, and it's generally a positive feeling, whether examined from the viewpoint of oneself or others. When we express sincere appreciation, we do so through humility.

As a result, the expression of gratitude through appreciation presents the potential for very real and tangible impact, and it should probably go without even stating it, but people like to feel appreciated. Research shows that people who feel valued and appreciated have markedly increased positive and optimistic attitudes, which then leads them to a greater chance of performing for the sake of self-satisfaction rather than pursuit of an extrinsic or monetary result. This probably means that we didn't need to start the monthly incentive program at our not-so-little retail establishment, and if anything, it may have diluted our gratitude experiment. It's a complete and utter no-fucking-brainer to state that people lose motivation if the beneficiaries of their efforts fail to acknowledge their labor by handing over a bit of appreciation. Even the tiniest bit of gratitude expressed for a kindness or ovation goes a long fucking way toward positively reinforcing more of that action in the future by maintaining a positive relationship with that other person.

When we express appreciation regularly, then research shows that we, as givers, can expect a number of benefits, such as better capacity for restful sleep, far stronger emotional resilience, greater optimist tendencies, and above all else, relational stability and satisfaction. That expression also earns social capital, and although this may seem like a totally selfish benefit, let's face it: who the fuck doesn't want to stow away favor for a rainy day?

Still, there seems to be an outbreak of spoiled-ass, rotten, entitled idiots who don't know how to fucking show their appreciation for even some of the most obvious things. These people are so wrapped up in their tiny fucking screens that, as life slips past them, so does every opportunity to express appreciation and nurture those relationships. That's why, in this chapter, our focus is going to be on putting the fucking phone down so that we might wake some of our brothers and sisters the fuck up.

### Chapter Challenge: Guerrilla Gratitude

Confession time: this activity gets me abso-fucking-lutely giddy. It's a social experiment on a small scale and takes very little investment on behalf of the experimenter, but good lord, the potential for impact is seriously fucking mammoth-sized. Ready for it?

Grab a stack of sticky notes and a pen. If you want to add some spicy sauce to the activity, dress up like a ninja, but that part isn't required. It's only in fun.

Then, look for even the slightest and most miniscule reason to thank the people in your daily orbit. Write those people thank-you notes, but don't sign them and don't leave any fucking indication it was you who did so. Place your sticky note in a conspicuous location where you know the person will easily find it, but do it without being seen. Don't post about it on social media, either, even if the only people who would see it is everyone other than the recipient. Your mission, you all-powerful, ever-silent, super appreciation ninja, is to secretly and quietly thank the people in your life, and I do mean as many of those people in one day as humanly possible. Here's a handful of ideas to get you started:

- Thank the custodian for keeping your building or floor tidy.
- Thank the cashier for putting up with awful, horrible people all day.
- Thank the stockperson for keeping shelves full.
- Thank your boss for having your back.
- Thank your coworkers for their moral support.
- Thank the person who considerately parked between the lines.
- Thank the cart person for braving the elements to round up shopping carts and protect our cars from door dings in the parking lot.
- Thank a police officer, firefighter, meter reader, or mail carrier.
- Thank your neighbor for being quiet and staying the fuck out of your business (but be nicer than that).
- Thank your children for loving you unconditionally.
- Thank your spouse or partner for putting up with your annoying ass.

- Thank a friend for being willing to listen to your whiny ass.
- Thank a teacher for her or his dedication and patience with your disruptive ass.
- Thank a sibling for helping you to live to see adulthood.
- Thank a parent for not eating you alive when you were young.

Your challenge here is to run out of an entire fucking stack of sticky notes in just one day. If you are successful in this endeavor, spend a bit of time reflecting at the end of the day on how it felt to do so. Did it elevate your mood? Did any of the recipients tell you about the notes, and if so, how hard was it to shut the hell up and not own up to the activity? Did any of them figure out it was you, and if so, what was that like?

What we're trying to accomplish with this activity is the isolation of one aspect of expressing appreciation, and that is the side of the giver. With a typical expression of appreciation, there's a complex web of interaction that activates mirror neurons in our brain. Once we express appreciation, it automatically causes the recipient to intuitively and instinctively reciprocate the ovation, so if we do this anonymously, then it short-circuits this process and allows us, the givers, to focus solely on the reaction we experience as a result of expressing our gratitude. If we're lucky enough to have someone tell us about the mysterious note, then we can isolate the feeling even further by resisting the urge to fess up. This, my friends, distills and purifies the motivation behind appreciation, for we are not expressing it for the sole purpose of reciprocation, but rather for the sake of appreciation itself. Good lord, that's some profound shit, if I do say so myself.

It also gives us something to do that doesn't involve screens! In fact, I'd be willing to bet that, if you keep track of your screen time with an app like I do, then the day you're out and about with the sticky notes, your screen time will absolutely plummet. During this activity, you're activating the same reward center that you access when you feed your social media addiction, but instead of likes and comments, you're making a tangible fucking difference in someone's day, a difference that is felt, remembered, and potentially even spread outward like a ripple effect, long after the activity has ended.

# PART IV:

## PUT THE FUCKING PHONE DOWN & GET YOUR SHIT TOGETHER

Hot damn, last part of the book, here we come! Only four more chapters to bear through with me, your sanctimonious, holier-than-thou bullshit artist. Let's review what brought us up to this point:

- In the first part of the book (Chapters 1-3), we learned about the importance of self-awareness and how to go about nurturing that quality so that we can actually notice what's going on around ourselves. We learned about listening, as well as why being alone and bored isn't such a bad thing after all.
- In the second part (Chapters 4-7), which I'll admit probably wasn't all that fun, we stepped outside the comfort zones we've built up through our insular use of tiny fucking screens. We confronted criticism, expanded the boundaries of our comfort zones, admitted to being wrong and sought forgiveness for doing so, and conducted an emotional autopsy in pursuit of more vulnerability and accountability. Fuck, that was painful, but at the same time, oh-so-necessary.
- In part three (Chapter 8-11), we examined what to do with all that time and presence once we've nurtured more of it in our daily existence. We explored the concept of savoring and how learning to prolong enjoyment of life through anticipation, savoring the moment, and reminiscence after the fact can really fucking increase our overall happiness and wellbeing. Then, we flipped the switch on gratitude and appreciation by kicking off a daily gratitude practice (which you'd better still be doing every day) and getting devious with a pack of sticky notes.

In this, our final part and last four chapters together, our goal is to tie all this shit together in a pretty pink bow so that this becomes one of those gifts that keep on giving as we generate long-term changes to our behavioral habits.

We're going to kick things off by examining how we can better control what we consume. After all, our bodies are complex and advanced bio-machines, which kind of makes us sound like a type of bad-ass cyborgs or something. Suck it, Van Damme! These machines run on the fuel we put inside, which includes not only actual biofuel like food, drink, booze, and sunshine, but also what our minds consume. The first chapter in this part specifically looks at how we can go on sort of a meal plan for our brains by learning to consume only that which has value, thereby bringing us into balance with respect to social input. It's like a detox for the soul and a way we can take more control over what we read, see, and hear on a daily basis.

In the second chapter of this fourth part, we'll take a look at a concept I call the "share-erang," which is like a boomerang you can't hit people with, but instead, involves learning to create content and share it mindfully since we live in a 24/7/365.25 news cycle and timelines filled to the brim with oversharing. We'll also explore the impact comparison to others has on our mental health and how we can apply that to what we learned previously with respect to mindful consumption of social media.

For the third, penultimate chapter, we're going to explore what life might look like if we actually put our fucking phones down and started making this shithole of a world better, not only for ourselves, but for others as well. To accomplish this, we'll look closely at how to develop the characteristic of generosity, which is not only life-giving to the person being generous, but good fuck-gravy, does it make people smile faster than an unexpected government check. That shit is golden.

Finally, we'll discuss what it means to take back control like a motherfucking boss—control over our time, our attention, and how we interact within our most important relationships. We'll have so much fucking control that Janet Jackson will sue each one of us for copyright infringement. Kids, if you don't get that joke, go ask your parents.

We'll lastly tie together each of the most important lessons from this entire fucking book so that you have a solid idea of where to go once that last page is turned. To do so, we'll learn to let go of what we can't control, accept what we can, and reclaim our rightful place in this life without a fucking phone in front of our faces every waking second.

# 12

## YOU ARE WHAT YOU CONSUME

Remember only a few pages ago or so when I mentioned that this chapter would be sort of like a diet for our relationship with technology? Every day, we consume a gargantuan ass-load of information. Marketing research estimates that the average American is exposed to anywhere from 4000 to 10,000 persuasive messages a day via various forms of electronic media. Granted, we simply can't pay attention to that many, or our brains would fucking explode, but it's still there. People who live in larger metropolitan areas may be exposed to even more than a redneck surfing porn in his mother's basement in rural Utah. Yes, Jethro, I'm talking about you. We know.

Aside from all the cheap plastic shit hocked online, we're also exposed to a fuck-freight of messages from others, from people meaninglessly bitching about their in-laws, to others posting every last fucking inane thing they do all day, to that one guy from high school who won't shut the fuck up about the great deals he can give you on life insurance. Communication is everywhere, and when we give it our attention, then it means we're consuming it, much in the same way we fork-shovel our gobs with deep-fried carnie fare at least once a year. Therefore, it fucking behooves us to mind more of what we consume, because inevitably and like it or despise it, that shit *will* affect us and the way we perceive the world surrounding us. The goal of this chapter is to provide a few practical tools and techniques as a series of steps for the purpose of trimming the bullshit and keeping behind only the good stuff. Think of these three steps as this chapter's challenges, but as with everything else buried within this tome, it begins with putting the fucking phone down.

## Step 1: Digital Detox

Just now, as well as the better part of the past 50,000 or so words, I've nagged the piss out of you to put the fucking phone down and do _____, probably to the point where it's drilled into your brain if you're still reading and haven't ditched my book in favor of a Netflix binge. Of course, it's all fun and games until we actually try to put the fucking phone down and fail as miserably as a lawnmower running on grape-flavored Kool Aid. It doesn't matter how much sugar you keep adding to that shit, it's not going anywhere, and your lawn will still look like hell.

I teach a college course to students interested in exploring the way social media has changed the dynamics of interaction online, and every semester, I ask them to do something only their parents have ever asked (more likely forced) them to do: absolutely NO social media for an entire week! Funny enough, even though most of them fail spectacularly about halfway through a single week and act like they're sneaking a hit of Twitter or getting their Insta-fix like a goddamn crackhead, at the end of the semester, I always ask what their favorite activity was of the course. Inevitably, the majority say it was the no-social week that really pumped their nads, to paraphrase Bender from The Breakfast Club. Why in the crystalline fucknuts is it so bloody hard to put our phones down? I think that question is best addressed using yet another story, and this one is one of my faves.

## Story Time!

The year was 2008 when I found myself standing at a crossroads. The moment in question took place on a Saturday that started out like any other Saturday in my home. Everyone slept in a bit later than normal, followed by my wife and I feening for our caffeine fix, but then, we took a detour from the norm when we took our children with us to Costco.

And, there it is: Right there, I've given you every fucking reason in the world not to listen to anything else I have to write, based solely on my obviously questionable life choices. I mean, who in the blistering shitlord takes their ass to Costco on a Saturday, other than apparently, the rest of the civilized world?

About one month before what is now known as the "infamous Costco incident," I had purchased my first smart phone: a CrackBerry. This device was my attempt to liberate myself from the 8-10 soul-sucking hours a day I spent staring at a computer screen. After all, I always joked with my students that teaching is my joy, my passion, what I love, and quite possibly, what I would do for free (j/k, if you're one of my administrators reading this), but how do I earn my paycheck? That's done by answering emails and going to meetings that could have easily been avoided with a strategically worded email. Again, fuck meetings, right?

While the CrackBerry definitely couldn't get me out of all those meetings (and there is seriously a four-wheel drive fuck-barrow full of meetings in my average week), it definitely helped with email, because I immediately noticed I was spending 3-4 hours less each day behind a computer, which made me think: *Holy shit, this is awesome! Look at all this time I get to spend with my family*!

The problem was, my workload hadn't changed a bit. I had simply traded big screen time for small screen time, and because that small screen followed me around everywhere I fucking went, my work life started bleeding into my family time.

On that fateful day at Costco, somewhere between an obnoxiously large bag of dog food to feed our unnaturally large animals and a family-size box of orange chicken, I felt that ever-familiar buzz up against my leg: the notification of a new email! Without thinking, like a good Pavlovian dog, I wiped the drool from my mouth, retrieved my phone from my pocket, and read the email while I pushed the big-ass orange flatbed cart down the frozen foods aisle. You can probably guess what happened next.

Moments later, the cart came to a sudden and abrupt halt. As I continued looking down at my phone, I immediately calculated that, given the average population density of Costco on a Saturday, the odds were astronomically large that I had just collided with another human. Nervously, I looked up, and that's when I saw that I'd hit my wife.

Say it with me, people, out loud and slowly: Fuck.

With her arms crossed and looking down the rim of her glasses at me, the next words out of her mouth were, "Put the fucking phone down." And now, you know where I got the name of this book. This story is where it all began, kids.

Our collision kicked off a series of rather spirited negotiations for the remainder of that day, and, of course, by negotiations, I mean, we fought like our fucking lives depended upon winning some bejeweled imaginary argument belt from the World Argument Federation. I defended myself by arguing that I *needed* to check my phone at any time so that I could be responsive to my students and colleagues. From my point of view, once I had freed myself from the shackles of my computer desk and started spending more time with my family, my job was done. Jesus, I sound like such a fucking wanker here, and in all honesty, it was not one of my prouder moments.

We all know there's a Grand Canyon-sized difference between merely occupying the same air space as another human like a piece of furniture or a goddamned potted plant and being fully present and emotionally available like someone who actually gives a flying fuck about the outcome of that moment. Even as I tell this story now, I'm embarrassed to admit that I was sending my wife the message that my students and colleagues mattered more to me than the time I should have been giving her. Every motherhumping time I reached for my phone when we were together, I was essentially placing our relationship on hold.

The result of our heated negotiations was a fairly simple solution at first glance. My wife kindly acknowledged the Sisyphean task of managing my email, so she asked one teensy-weensy little thing of me: One day, 24 hours, every week, with no fucking screen in front of my face whatsoever. We got our whole family involved, and we even gave it a catchy nickname (Screen-Free Saturday™) to make it seem more like a challenge. On Friday night, we agreed to put all phones, tablets, and computers away, and we wouldn't touch them again until Sunday morning. It was our way of trying to meaningfully reconnect with one another in the real world without all the distractions of the virtual world tugging at our attention spans.

Although this deal was simple and acted as our compromise, if I'm being honest, I was freaking the fuck out. I mean, if I had a hard time getting all my shit done in seven days, how in the blessed fuck was I going to get it done in six? On that first Screen-Free Saturday™, it was like I had just quit smoking, which, by the way, I had already quit two years prior to the infamous Costco incident, so I knew how intensely fucking hard that shit is to put down.

But, on this particular Saturday, I had some seriously heinous withdrawal symptoms, like my pocket suddenly growing a mysterious gravitational field that drew my hand into its orbit to check the empty space where my phone used to be every 10 seconds or so. My rock bottom was finding myself in the bathroom behind a locked door, sitting on the edge of the tub, with my face buried in my phone in secret. That was the moment I realized maybe I had a problem.

Did you notice that I'm using terms and phrases associated with addiction? That's fully intentional, because a recent study in the Journal of Behavioral Addiction concluded that screen addiction has become the single most motherfucking pervasive non-drug addiction facing our society and time. I just had a thought: Wouldn't it be awesome if academic journals allowed profanity? I'd read them so much more often if they did. Anyway, because of the rise of this addiction, we're seeing new problems emerge, like nomophobia (the fear of being without one's phone), phubbing (using our phones like an ostrich uses sand, to avoid social interaction with others around us), and FOMO (the fear that, if I leave social media for too long, then I'll miss out on something great).

These problems drive us all to some seriously jacked-up obsessive-compulsive behaviors, and they create a sense of urgency that, for many, feels as strong as the need for food, water, or even fucking air. Maybe that's why they call it a 'news feed,' because the most popular social media platforms are intentionally designed around our innate desire to connect with other humans. Bad-ass dad jokes aside, our brains reward us with a little chemical shot of feel-good hormones like dopamine for seeking out those connections, and it doesn't matter if this happens online or in-person. Every time we feel a buzz, hear a ding, or see that stupid fucking little red notification number perched precariously and conspicuously atop of an app icon, they act as triggers that mindlessly suck us in like a goddamn tractor beam on the Death Star, and it isn't until we're hooked and try to break free that we realize the sheer power of these impulses.

As I sat on the edge of the tub on that first Saturday and wallowed in the personal shame I felt for hiding my insane behavior from my family, I resolved to commit to my own digital detox. Within the next month of Screen-Free Saturdays™, I started to see the benefits emerge.

First, I was slowly re-learning how to control my entrance and exit to the digital world on my own motherfucking terms and in my own goddamn time. By doing so, I started becoming increasingly aware of all the countless, mindless urges I felt to check my phone: in line at the store, stopped at a red light, waiting at the doctor's office, etc. With that newfound awareness, it became easier for me to resist most of those urges and control my attention. During the other six days of the week, this helped me focus, like times when my priority should have been to listen to someone or in moments where I needed to simply notice and savor life as it happened, before I missed it all together.

Second, think about this: We all have the same 24 hours in a day; there's no dispute. Maybe if you're an astronaut orbiting high above the planet, time works a bit differently, but it's negligible. On this planet, when we willingly and openly choose to spend 24 hours of uninterrupted and undistracted time with our loved ones each week, that choice sends them a strong, clear message that reaffirms their top rank within our life's priorities. That shit right there goes a seriously long fucking way toward healthy relationships, even if none of the other benefits were present.

Third, I now recognize the symptoms of boredom and the urge to relieve that boredom. As mentioned way back in Chapter 3, all too often, we avoid boredom because of the discomfort and tension that comes with it, but when we automatically reach for our phones, we're shortchanging ourselves out of our higher levels of creative thought. For example, on one particularly rainy Screen-Free Saturday™, my kids and I were going a bit stir crazy because we'd done ALL the things. After sitting with my boredom for a while, I got the most amazing idea, seemingly out of nowhere. I rounded up all the cardboard I could find and asked my kids what they would like to build, if they could build anything in the world. After denying them of the rights to build a space shuttle, a whisky still, and a real live pony, we built a working skee-ball game in our basement out of nothing but cardboard, duct tape, and a whole fuck-load of imagination.

That day is still one of our top five favorite memories together. If I had mindlessly reached for my fucking phone at the first sign of boredom, it probably would never have happened. And, yes, I did record it on video with my phone on a fucking Saturday so we could remember it forever, so don't be so damn judgmental. The only guilt I feel is for not recording it in landscape mode instead of portrait mode, like good video should be. The goal of detoxing is not to adhere to some totalitarian set of rules like we're in communist Russia. It isn't like my wife slapped my hand every time I reached for my phone on a Saturday. Okay, maybe that happened twice, but I had it coming — both times. The goal of a digital detox each week is to learn to make deliberate choices regarding our attention because choice is what allows *us* to use our technology, rather than allowing *it* to control us. Opportunities like this will arise, but as long as we make exceptions from a place of deliberate choice rather than automatic impulse, then the activity still fulfills its purpose.

One of the coolest apps I know in existence are those that measure and report our screen time and usage. When Apple released their version in 2018, I don't think a lot of people were ready for the results, and by a lot of people, I mean every-fucking-body with an iPhone. The New York Post reported that the average American screen time, as of November 2018, clocked in at around seven un-fucking-believable hours a day. Think about that. That's nearly half of our waking existence spent staring at these tiny fucking screens while life passes us by, completely unnoticed.

From November 2018 to February 2019, I was pleasantly surprised to learn that my daily average didn't peak over 2.5 hours a day—not perfect, because, let's face it, I still need my phone, and I still love my phone, but my average represents more of a balanced usage. Could I do better? Sure, if I kept pushing it, but I'm constantly reassessing myself by checking in with loved ones about my phone usage (see the Blind Spot activity in Chapter 4). BTW, I was totally wrong before when I speculated that I wouldn't be able to get all my work done in six days. Now, I'm getting far more done with even less time, because that one day off each week allows me to refine and sharpen my focus to resist distractions, which helps me use the time I have much more efficiently.

I know I sound like some kind of arrogant asshole, bragging like, "Ooh, look at my fancy, super-low screen-free time," but this simple activity works for a reason. On top of my decreased screen time, my 15-year-old daughter, who should hypothetically average somewhere around 9-10 hours a day like the rest of her peers, consistently averages less than three hours a day, and that's when I was hit by a blinding realization. Even though my quest to control mindless impulses and invest in my relationships was motivated out of self-preservation (I was worried my wife might strangle me someday if I didn't get my shit together, especially if I ever hit her again with a cart), the fact that our family did it together, leading to my kids growing up in this environment, it led us to a drastic cultural shift, even in the face of outside social influences.

After 10 years of digital detoxing, the most important thing I've learned is that I will never fucking remember my very best day spent staring at my phone.

When I stood at those crossroads 10 years ago, faced with the decision to either continue allowing my attention to aimlessly wander from one little red notification number to the next, or to commit to stepping away from the screen to invest in my face-to-face relationships, I'm so glad I listened to my wife and put my fucking phone down. Doing so has made my relationships stronger, my interactions more meaningful, and all the memories created with my loved ones have had a significantly higher resolution than any screen could ever provide.

But, the best part is that I have hit far fewer loved ones with a big orange flatbed cart on a busy Saturday at Costco.

Thank you for coming to my TED talk.

Actually, no shit, that really *was* my TED talk, delivered at TEDx Coeur d'Alene in January of 2019.

Except for all the profanity.

They wouldn't let me.

Trust me, I asked.

Twice.

### Step 2: Feed-icure

In 1968, a bad-ass communication super-professor, George Gerbner, established the Cultural Indicators Research Project, which analyzed television programming for over a decade in an attempt to understand the effect it had on viewers. This legendary project not only discovered that children's programming contained the highest rates of violence per minute by far, but it also identified types of people most likely to be victims of violence. Guess who? Women and minorities. Beyond the rich data telling us what we're watching all the time, Gerbner also coined a fascinating concept, the *Mean World Syndrome*, which showed how consuming too much television could potentially convince a person to believe the world is significantly more dangerous than it really is, thanks to the higher rates of violence portrayed on television.

It's not hard to imagine that, if someone consistently watches 10 hours of cable news a day, they're probably going to piss themselves at the thought of running an errand to the fucking post office. After all, there's an old familiar saying in journalism that, if it bleeds, it leads. Guerrilla gratitude, as seen in Chapter 11, won't exactly make news unless it's a human-interest story they plug in at the end of the show as filler or a palate cleanser after all the murder-death-kills they reported beforehand. But here's the real shit-splitter: Gerbner found that the rate of media consumption that tipped the scales toward such a batshit crazy-town view of the world was around six or seven hours of TV a day. Hmm, where have we seen a similar number? Oh yeah, remember when I mentioned that the current average American screen time is nearly seven fucking hours a day?

Say it with me again, people, out loud and slowly: Fuck.

Think about it. As we gravitate toward a rate of media consumption encompassing nearly half our waking existence, that media shapes our assumptions of life all around us. If all I'm reading are articles on the crumbling decay of democracy or how fucking racist, sexist, ageist, ableist, or any other isms that are dominating the world around me, then that's going to taint my presuppositions of the world as I leave the house. Suddenly, everyone is a potential aggressor, asshole, or enemy, and if I view them as such, then I'm probably going to be a bit edgy. Remember the kid with the hammer? Yeah, that's us on too much social media, and suddenly, every-fucking-thing becomes a nail.

Therefore, I propose a feed-icure, which is like a manicure but instead of the keratin growing from our fingertips, we use it on the algorithms controlling what we read, see, and hear on a daily basis. If we use Step 1 from earlier in the chapter to detox regularly, then we'll reduce our screen time eventually, but it isn't all that likely that we're going to eliminate it, because, well, phones are fucking cool, and so is social media for the most part. That reduction in screen time will help, but our next step is to ensure that any remaining screen time is well spent.

If you're not familiar with social media's algorithms, here's a super quick and dirty tour. An algorithm is a pattern of predictable behavior. Our phones, tablets, computers, smart TVs, etc., are all designed to show us what they "think" we like, based on our usage history. If I head over to Amazon and start searching for diabetic compression socks and syringes, it won't be long before I see my social media feeds respond by showing me a bunch of shit related to diabetes. These algorithms are designed to keep us scrolling for as long as possible, because the more we scroll, the more ads we'll see, and the more ads the social media platform can show its users, the more the company has to pay to run its ads. In the end, the advertisers win, thanks to greater visibility, the social platform wins all the way to the fucking bank, but I'm not so sure us users win anything at all. In fact, I think we're pretty much fucked. The more we scroll, the more potential damage we do to our perceptions of the world around us, if we subscribe to Gerbner's research. But, goddammit, we're going to know right where to fucking order those polka-dot compression socks with the cute-ass pugs all over them.

Here's the cool bit: Algorithms are a computer program. They will only do as they're told, so we can effectively control what they show us, once we know how to do so. For example, Facebook has pretty simple algorithm controls that allow us to hide the shit we don't like, unfollow racist uncles around election time, block the assholes we don't know, and create friend groups that allow us to tailor exactly what we see. Other platforms have similar controls to varying degrees, but in the end, it all comes down to us and the wrench-time we put in to curating a more positive and user-friendly feed.

Instead of mindlessly scrolling and absorbing every piece of content that flies by as we do, we have a choice to make, and when we make those choices, we are able to manicure our feeds to ensure what we see when we scroll is exactly what we deliberately and intentionally *choose* to see. It simply requires a bit of input at first.

For every piece of content that we see, we should assess its value at that moment, and as Marie Kondo asks, does it bring you joy? Actually, maybe joy is the wrong word to use here. Does it have value to you? More to the point, try to identify if that content is sensational and designed to elicit a negative emotional reaction from you. If so, trim and cut that fucker.

For ads that don't add this kind of value to your experience, take a moment to hide it by clicking on the menu associated with that post. That tells the algorithm that this isn't something you want to see.

For friends' or followers' posts, take the time to hide them as well. Some platforms give you even more options, such as "snoozing" friends for a set period or unfollowing them, which still leaves them as a connection that you can check in on later, but unfollowing allows you to check in on them when *you* want, instead of having their bullshit in your face all the time.

If you have friends or followers who present a toxic threat to your experience, fucking unfriend and/or block those motherfuckers. Trust me on this. It's okay. Doing so doesn't murder the person in real life. You can still talk to that person using other means, if you must. It simply means you don't want them cluttering up your social feed. In fact, my sister-in-law even told her mom, my mother-in-law, that she refuses to be friends with her on Facebook. It's not personal; it's merely a way of setting boundaries.

A lot of professors I know won't friend or follow their students on social media, which is totally their prerogative and one I completely understand. They keep a tight lid on their shit. Me? I find it nearly impossible to give even half a fuck. I'll connect with whomever wants to put up with my bullshit, and when they leave, I try not to take offense. However, when they do connect with me, I'll do a quick feed assessment to see if I think they're compatible with my particular brand of bullshit, and if not, I'll set up controls so that I get to manage what they do and do not see.

The point here is that *we* take control over what we're being fed on social media. Sure, the algorithm is creepy as fuck, I'll admit, like when I don't even search for something and I magically start seeing ads after merely *thinking* about the topic. But, as mentioned, it's only software, so we can manipulate it nearly as much as it manipulates us. It only takes a bit of time and effort to set up and maintain.

Emotional contagion is real. Our attitudes affect those in our orbits, and theirs affect ours as well. If I feed-icure my experience to where I'm seeing mostly positive, feel-good stories and content, then I'm likely to start absorbing a lot of that positivity, which then impacts my offline life as well. If I allow the negativity in, and it starts creeping in pervasively, then it certainly has the potential to impact my mood negatively as well. We'll cover a lot more of this concept later, in Chapter 13.

### Step 3: Pick a Fight

I believe Tyler Durden said it best when he stated, "I want you to hit me as hard as you can." These immortal words from *Fight Club* kicked off a series of events in one of the greatest mind-fuck movies of all time, and like Tyler, I have a homework assignment for you. I want you to pick a fight.

Hold up! Hang on a second before you put the book down and go looking for some ass to kick. The fight I want you to pick is not with a random stranger; it's with someone you know, or rather, *some thing.* I want you to pick a fight with your routine.

First, come up with a basic list of your daily rituals and routines, and be really fucking detailed with it. The more detailed you are, the easier these fights will be to pick. Here's mine, for example:

- Alarm at 6:00 AM.
- Snooze until 6:09 AM.
- Snooze until 6:18 AM.
- Snooze until 6:27 AM.
- Groan like a little bitch about how much I hate mornings.
- Pick up my phone and check for lock-screen notifications, even though I don't have my glasses on and can't see them anyway.
- Unlock my phone and look at how many emails I received from all those east-coast bastards who are already on their third cup of coffee.
- Sit up.
- Groan some more.
- Stand up.
- Let the big idiot dog outside.
- Let the annoying little dog outside.

- Yell at my daughter to wake up.
- Wake up my son in the most annoying way possible.
- Procure caffeine.
- Take a shower.
- Get dressed.
- Brush teeth.
- Put on deodorant.
- Ask kids if they're ready yet.
- Get bag together.
- If winter, start car, defrost windows, and get those heated seats warming up.
- Sit on sofa and space off for about 10 minutes.
- Gather children, get in the car, and go.

Okay, this little window into my life is the first hour of my every weekday during the regular school year. If I wanted to pick a fight with my routine, I could choose literally any bullet point from that list and challenge myself to do it differently.

- I could pick a fight with my alarm by getting up without hitting snooze.
- I could REALLY challenge myself to get up earlier so I could drink my coffee while watching the sun rise. Shit, that sounds good, but double-puss-bucket, it sounds difficult.
- I could refuse to even look at my phone until I get to work.
- I could wake up my kids with Nerf guns. Hmm, that sounds like a plan for tomorrow.
- I could get dressed and *then* take a shower. Actually, that sounds uncomfortable.

I'm sure you get the idea. The point is to acknowledge our typical routines by first making a list and then picking a fight with those things throughout each day. Do this for a week, and I guaran-fucking-tee you that it will pay off.

Picking fights like this is a way to jumpstart our creative process. Not only does it form new neural pathways in our brains, but the activity forces us to question our routines. It yanks us right the fuck out of our assumed norms and places us into a novel position, which, if you'll recall, is one of the components of mindful presence. Believe it or not, something as simple as picking a fight with an alarm clock can generate and nurture mindful presence for us when we need it most.

As we get stuck in routines, we generate a system of assumptions and expectations without even realizing it, and these can quickly pose a threat to our ability to adapt to life as it happens. The stronger our attachment to these expectations and assumptions, the harder it becomes to adapt when something gets in the way of what we expect. However, after picking fights with these elements of our routine, we're actually developing a more agile and flexible orientation toward change, as well as sparking our creative energy. That strengthened orientation toward change can later reduce fear and anxiety associated with change, moving us toward more nonjudgmental acceptance of the moment as it unfolds, which is yet another aspect of mindful presence.

## Chapter Challenge: Diet for the Mind

As the great Shia LeBeouf once exclaimed in front of a green screen, "Do it! Just do it!" Try the three steps outlined in this chapter for a while as a means of detoxing your mind, but instead of diet that involves trimming out yummy things like bread, sugar, bacon, bread, meat, bread, fatty foods, bacon, and, of course, bread & bacon together, we're taking control over behavior and the way we interact with the world around us.

Start by picking a day throughout the week to detox and remove yourself from screen time, whether that's a Tech-Free Tuesday, Phone-Free Friday, or Wi-Fi-Less Wednesday. Pick a day and stick to it. It may take a month or so to start noticing results, but I promise you, they *will* come with time and commitment. Then, you'll start noticing how much others are on their phones, and it will annoy the piss out of you more and more. Suggest this book to them, and when they get to this chapter, they'll be like, "That asshole! She/he gave me this book because I'm one of *those* people, huh?" And it will be cool, because you will know deep down in your heart that you were right, and there's nothing these people can do about it. Cool.

Then, clean up your feed. This will also take time, as most platforms' feeds are designed to ignore anomalies, so a one-time shot won't do it. The more you hide, unfollow, block, and remove, the cleaner your feed will become, and eventually, you'll be left with something you can live with as you scroll.

Finally, pick fights with your ruts, routines, and regular assumed norms. Do it for at least a week and then incorporate such fights into part of your regular life. And then, pick a fight with that as well, once the fights become part of the routine. Keep yourself on your toes, and your future self will thank you for it. Hell, pick fights with your fucking toes. Shifty little bastards, aren't they?

This isn't keto, paleo, or whatever-the-fuck fad diet is popular by the time you read this. These are principles that make real, tangible differences in real-time—differences you can feel and others will notice and appreciate.

Just think: you don't even have to deprive yourself of bacon or bread to make it happen.

# 13
# THE SHARE-ERANG

When I was a kid, I wanted a boomerang so fucking bad. Seems like I always saw them advertised near the back of my favorite comic books, and each time, I'd dream of getting the money together to order one, presuming the organization I sent my money to would actually follow through and deliver me my exotic Australian wonder stick. Sadly, I never made that happen, but during my teen years, I just so happened to run across a wooden boomerang at a novelty store, and all that nostalgic yearning came flooding back. I sprung something like 20 bucks for it, and I couldn't get my ass to a park fast enough to test it. I read the directions carefully, which told me to throw it with plenty of spin while throwing it at about a 45-degree angle. Beaming with delight and childlike wonder, I chucked that fucker with all my might, standing in the midst of a rundown baseball field by my house.

Guess what? I never saw the fucking thing in one piece again. It flew away from me, spinning like a helicopter rotor, defying its originally designed purpose by maintaining an arrow-straight trajectory toward the baseball backstop. It struck the upper end of the fencing structure and busted into more pieces than dollars it cost for me to experience such a regrettable and heinous mistake.

Completely unlike my childhood boomerang (which I'm still apparently bitter about), the information that we share to the digital world is guaranteed to come back to us in one form or another, regardless of what angle we happen to post at or the 'spin' we put on it. This is why I've assigned the title of "the Share-erang" to this chapter.

There's a fascinating theory within communication studies called social penetration theory (yeah, I know — it sounds naughty) that explains a lot about our in-person interactions. You may have even heard this theory referenced in a famous movie about a big green ogre who lived in a swamp and hung around with a talking donkey. Yeah, that's the one. "Ogres are like onions" right? Social penetration theory (stop laughing and focus) suggests that people also have layers, and as we get to know others, we dive deeper and deeper into those layers. At first, people might discuss names, occupations, where they're from, their basic interests, and so on. Typically, we'll save conversations about shit like politics and religion until we've covered everything from the outer layers first.

But, something funny happens when we go online. All too often, we forget this interactional norm when there's a screen between us and them. In fact, fuck social norms, right? Politics and religion? Fuck yeah! Let's all discuss our most deeply-held personal beliefs with utter strangers online! Furthermore, it's perfectly acceptable to call someone I've never met a filthy socialist commie or a gun-loving ammosexual while hiding behind a keyboard.

Can you imagine if we behaved in person how we so often behave online? Imagine this situation: I'm standing in line at the grocery store with a cold soda, a bag of chips, and some dish soap, when I notice the person in front of me is wearing a shirt with a political slogan on it. I drop my shit, shove the person from behind, and yell like I'm stuck in caps lock: "HEY ASSHOLE! GO BACK TO CALIFORNIA! YOUR NOT WELCOME AROUND HERE!" Yes, the misspelling was intentional, though I'm not sure how I'd screw up the difference between *your* and *you're* in vocal speech the same way so many ignorant assholes fuck it up online. You think that situation would end well for me? Probably not, given my complete and utter inadequacy for physical violence. I can't simply block someone in real life who's winding up for an uppercut, standing directly in front of me.

If we wouldn't do this in person, then why do it online? The answer seems somewhat obvious. People feel empowered when removed from physical immediacy. Once there's a keyboard between us and them, and we remove all potential for physical endangerment, then we feel free to communicate any old idiotic thought that comes to mind. If you ever doubt this, simply post something – *anything* – to Facebook, the place where humans go to find out how truly wrong they are – about any-fucking-thing. Therefore, now is a really great time for us to discuss the concept of mindful sharing, or put more simply, the act of thinking critically about the value behind what we share.

Within the confines of the social media class I teach, one of the main principles I discuss is this idea of mindful sharing. I ask both my own children and my students to consider one simple question before everything they post: Would you feel comfortable explaining the content or intent behind your post to a parent, partner, spouse, boss, a reporter, or a jury? If the answer to any of those is no, then you should either reconsider posting that particular content or find a way to limit your audience to only those who might benefit from such content. As for me and the constant torrent of bullshit I tend to share on social media, I'm good with it, though I can only imagine how uncomfortably odd it would be to explain many of my posts to a jury, depending on the context of the court case in question.

The point of this, and the idea behind the share-erang, is to consider the potential impact of whatever we share, particularly in light of how it might come back to us in another form. In the same manner in which we need to consider what we consume (see Chapter 12) as a function of how that consumption affects our perception of the world, we need to consider the impact left behind from what we put out into the world. Whatever we put out, *will* come back. It's merely a question of when. The same algorithms governing our feeds gorge themselves not only off of what we like, comment on, and share or retweet, but also off of our original content. If I start posting critiques of Congress, not only would I have unlimited material from which to draw upon, but the algorithm would adjust accordingly and assume I'm interested in a certain brand of politics.

It isn't merely the algorithm affected by what we post; all those who subscribe to what we post are potentially impacted even further. For onlookers, what we post paints a picture of the kind of person I am, and social media spectators constantly fill in the blanks when information is missing, so even partially posting a specific topic consistently will lead others to form a certain impression.

Sometimes, we might post out of frustration in hopes that others will come rushing to our aid, reminding us that it will be okay. Everyone does this once in a while, except those perfect fuckers who never have any problems, and they're the ones we love to hate. However, if we do this each and every fucking day of the week, then guess what? Fewer and fewer friends will come to our aid, and before we know it, we don't receive as many invites to movie night or anything else for that matter because everyone thinks of us as whiny little bitches. In reality, maybe we simply weren't aware of the impression we were giving off, which is why it is so bloody important for us to keep a mindful eye on the overall subject matter we post.

### Chapter Challenge #1: Audit the Feed

Using your platform of choice, take a moment to audit what you post (i.e., your timeline, tweets, feed, etc.). Go back at least a month, if not more, and try to look at your posts as an outsider. As you read through them, imagine yourself being a brand-new friend or follower and think critically about the impression your feed presents. Consider creating a table or scorecard system, where you rank the positivity or negativity of each post from an outsider's point of view. Then, add it all up and determine if your impression comes across as overwhelmingly positive or negative. You might be surprised, whether pleasantly or less-than-pleasantly, once the numbers are in, so be prepared for an awakening, rude or otherwise.

Or not. That's okay, too.

Still, this marks the first step in becoming more aware of our potential impact on others within our social circle and learning to take control over how we are seen by others.

## The Thief of Joy

You might have read or heard the famous quote from Teddy Roosevelt, "Comparison is the thief of joy." The first time I heard it, I was dumbfounded, partially because of how much wisdom is densely packed into a simple six-word phrase. Most of the times in my life where I've felt inadequate occurred when I was comparing myself to others who I viewed as significantly smarter, better-looking, more powerful, wiser, talented, or successful. They always seemed to have it all and carried themselves far more confidently than I could ever dream. The comparison seemed so objective and infallible that I never dared question the conclusions I drew from such comparison.

Along came social media, and now every-fucking-body is comparing their shit to one another in real time. I was a 28-year-old undergraduate when social media first exploded by way of MySpace. I peeked into the phenomenon, curious about why everyone was talking about it, and all of sudden, I felt more inadequate than ever before. In fact, I was a lowly fucking peon, unworthy of anything in my life if my comparisons were to be believed. Here I was, a husband and father of three racking up student loans and trying to change my life while being a role model to my kids, while comparing my impoverished life in a single-wide trailer to my peers, most of whom were in their late teens or early twenties. Their lives seemed so fucking colorful and exciting, filled with: hugs, smiles, drinks, and parties; short-term relationships, one night stands, concerts, and road trips; and laughs, memories, and inside jokes to which I was not privy. Suddenly, I felt more alone than I had ever felt in my entire goddamn life, and I was the punchline to all their old fart jokes.

Was that what was happening in reality? Fuck no! My peers were wonderful, caring friends who loved and respected me, were more than happy to have me around, and I continue to be friends with so very many of them to this day, more than 15 years later. The truth, however, was that I constantly compared the struggles of my life to the apparent joys of theirs. Too bad I didn't realize that what they shared online was only their highlight reels. Nobody shared the dark times, the loneliness, the hangovers, the breakups, the struggles to pay the rent, or how often they ended up stranded in a strange place with no way to get home on a Friday night. They were all too busy feeling like *they* had to keep up with their peers as well by outshining them and sharing all the best parts while feeling just as utterly fucking inadequate as I felt, but for totally different reasons.

I had to realize that social media was a mediated and manicured version of reality. That stunningly poetic picture on Instagram of a young woman doing a yoga handstand on the beach in front of crashing crystal-blue waves? If we expanded the borders of that picture, we'd see the friend, barely out of frame, holding up her friend's ankles. We'd see all the annoyed families with babies, changing their shitty diapers out in the open for all to share in the smell. We'd see the garbage strewn all over the beach, just out of the shot, and we'd see the *real* color of the brownish-green water that had been carefully edited to appear bluer. This is what the original poster wants the world to *see*, rather than presenting a faithful representation of what actually *is*.

Therefore, my advice in this chapter is to watch ourselves and how we react to others' amazing and beautiful posts. Sure, that moment may appear serene and picturesque, but we can't allow ourselves to compare current reality to this mediated reality, because what we see is likely curated or perhaps even fictional, which is a much nicer way of accusing people of lying. Trust me on this: the share-erang comes back for them as well. The further they drift away from their real-life experiences, the more they will need to lie to perpetuate the fantasy.

**Story Time!**

Many of us resort to curating our lives as a means to have something of interest to post, and I've found myself guilty of this on more than one occasion. One particular incident springs to mind, which involved the first day of school for my two youngest children. On the eve before the first day of school, which also happened to be my youngest son's first day of second grade at a new school, I spent the better part of an hour cuddled up next to him before bed, listening to him as he discussed his fears and worries with me, including everything from getting lost, to having a mean teacher, to dealing with playground assholes and worrying about whether the kids at the new school would accept him or not.

The following morning, after what I can only assume was a restless night since he woke up about two hours early, he had a bounce to his step, complete with a positive attitude and a sense of courage to head to his new school. When we got to school that morning, I parked about a block away so that he, my youngest daughter, and I could walk together and talk about any last-minute hesitations. We held hands and took our steps slowly, enjoying the crisp, late summer morning, and those last few moments of freedom before the bell tolled the official start of the school year.

Fucking hell, they were so young then.

We paused, right before entering the building so I could take our traditional first-day-of-school picture of my son and his sister. You know the shot. It's the one all our parent friends inevitably plaster all over their fucking timelines the first week of September. After taking the pic, we embraced tightly for one more hug, and I leaned down to give him a kiss, savoring the moment, knowing full well that, before long, those kisses and hugs in front of the school might likely disappear. As I watched my babies walk into the building, I sighed, feeling the melancholic release of yet another summer's memories slip away from my grasp, relegated solely to memory.

My "Hallmark moment" was interrupted by what I did next. Like a total asshole, I reached into my pocket, took out my phone, and as I walked, my focus shifted toward choosing the perfect settings on Instagram for the picture so I could show off my kids to all my friends and absorb the likes as they rolled in, thereby validating my worth as a parent. After I posted the picture, a strange sense of remorse crept in, and it dawned on me that, as of late (as of the last few years, really), I've been taking pictures of every fucking moment, from the trivial to the sublime, and everything in between.

I know for a fact that I'm not alone, seeing as how one of my favorite pastimes involves getting the family together, pulling up the hard drive, broadcasting it to the Apple TV, and going through each folder, month-by-month, and reminiscing and recounting stories of our favorite memories. Every time I took a pic of a family moment, it was like I was collecting data for future iterations of our collective reminiscence. But, there was something different about this moment. I began wondering if I had been "chasing memories" — deliberately manipulating our activities and behaviors so as to capture the perfect shot, the one that everyone in my friends list would ooh and ah over for days to come, as a result of crafting the perfect post.

The more pervasive social media became, the more frequently I sought out "photo ops" and suddenly, what used to be special moments became less about savoring the experience of being together and more about capturing the perfect light, the perfect pose, the perfect smile — the perfect mediated representation of how I want others to view my family. I began looking at life not as a series of moments to be treasured, but as images to be collected, edited, and republished for everyone to share. I had somehow drifted away from parenthood and more toward becoming the family photographer and social media director, and that wasn't how I wanted my kids to remember me when they looked back on their childhoods.

After this realization, I decided to try an experiment on myself later that afternoon. I arrived early to my kids' school to pick them up, where I took up residence on a rock wall under the flagpole, with the early September sun warming my back. As I glanced up, noticing the flag waving gently in the breeze and shimmering with translucence when it passed in front of the sun's rays, my immediate thought was about what a fucking awesome picture it would make for Instagram. I politely told my urge to fuck off and let it fade, leaving my phone parked within the folds of my pocket, and this act of letting go produced an involuntary, effortless smile.

As all the other parents arrived, I looked around, taking inventory of what I noticed. At least eight out of every ten parents had their faces buried in their fucking phones, while the remaining two of every ten were grandparents, who seemed serenely content to simply wait patiently, sans electronics. Their mere presence called back to an echo of a forgotten era, yet one strangely familiar. All of these grandparents displayed the same effortless grin that overcame me as well.

The bell rang, and the children filed out, their eyes darting back and forth as they scanned the faces in the crowd for their parents. As children's eyes locked with their respective parents, both squealed with delight before the kids' little legs sprinted across the concrete. As the parents whose faces were previously transfixed on their phones saw their kids, each and every fucking one of them affixed their phones to approximately one arm's length to prepare to capture a shot of their little ones running, whose arms remained outstretched in search of a greeting hug. Several of these parents couldn't get the moment captured in time before their kids reached them, and these people actually fucking ordered their children to back up and do it again! Of course, their children all rolled their eyes and sighed, and I remember thinking how ridiculous I would have felt in their shoes. Jesus, I'm so fucking glad phones weren't a thing when I was a kid.

Then, I saw my son walking out. Our eyes locked, and my smile became his. "Daddy!" he shouted gleefully, his arms stretched out before him, similar to all the other kids; however, without a phone occupying my hands, our arms actually met, locked together, and I swept him up, where I was met with one of the most memorable and joy-inducing hugs I've ever received. "Daddy, I missed you today," he whispered softly as his grip on my shoulders tightened and a euphoric chill crawled its way up every last fucking vertebra of my spine.

"I missed you too, buddy," I replied, "and I can't wait to hear you tell me about your first day on the way home."

Despite my profanity-enriched rants, I'm not a technophobe, believe it or not, and you'll never catch me advocating for the all-out destruction of smartphones, nor will you ever see me permanently deactivate my Facebook or Instagram accounts, much as I'd probably like to do so during election season. What I learned from this experiment was the difference between "chasing memories" and simply enjoying moments in the full resolution of life as those moments unfold. There are certainly times when a photo or video is necessary. Think of the big firsts: first steps, first day of kindergarten, first Christmas/birthday/date/drive, graduation etc. Those big-ass, super fucking important moments only come around once in a lifetime, and recording those moments for posterity makes sense.

But, all the other times? We seriously need to question our motivations more critically. We need to ask ourselves whether our attention would be better spent on capturing the moment with a pic or video or being an active fucking participant within that moment. Pictures may be fun to look at when we want to reminisce, but later in life, our children are much more likely to remember how they *felt* about the active roles we play in shaping such moments—something a picture can never fully replace. In the waning moments of one's life, I highly doubt anyone has ever regretted not taking enough pictures, and even if they had, I'm sure someone was around to tell that person to stop being such an asshole and fucking die already. I'm pretty damn certain there are plenty of people on their death beds who regretted not taking more time to be present with their loved ones. In fact, I'd almost be willing to make a fat bet that nearly everyone has that thought during their final moments, so perhaps it's never really enough.

On that experimental first day of school, seeing my kids somehow felt richer and more colorful. It was substantially more satisfying to me as a parent, and the memory of that moment has a significantly higher resolution than any screen could ever provide. Perhaps a picture or video would have afforded me the ability to revisit the moment repeatedly, but the memory I now carry in my mind is quite possibly the greatest picture I never took.

### Chapter Challenge #2: 24-Hour Hold

For your second of two challenges in this penultimate chapter of the book, I'm throwing down a pretty significantly life-altering challenge for you, but one that's pretty simple and doesn't require a lot of explanation. Simply put, every time you think about posting something to social media, stop yourself, wait 24 hours, and then decide if it's still worth posting. Do this for at least a week, if not longer. If your post involves bitching, moaning, whining, or complaining about something like political bullshit, bullshit in the news, or some bullshit that happened at work or whatever, wait 48 hours. Increase it to 72 hours if it's a really big deal.

Seriously, why in the holy fuck would I ask you to wait so long? The reason is that we all too often post without even thinking, and even more often, we do so hoping for social validation. Sometimes, we might even post simply because we're going through a temporary dopamine deficiency, and we need a boost. It's the brain's way of getting that fix we talked about earlier in the book. By building in an automatic delay process, we force ourselves to not only think more critically about what we post, but often times, we will end up posting a lot less frequently because, once the moment has passed, we come to realize how trivial or unimportant the post's content was in the first place. With more controversial topics, the added time allows us to consider our positions and the potential impact those thoughts may have upon others. It may even allow us to avoid unnecessary online flame wars that result in the inevitable loss of friends!

Ultimately, this act of defiance in the face of our typical urges allows us to gain greater control over that share-erang. Perhaps it won't shatter up against the proverbial backstop of our social network, leaving us sad and dejected.

And yes, I'm still bitter about that stupid fucking boomerang.

# 14

# DO SOMETHING WORTH REMEMBERING

Once upon a time, I had a freshman who wanted to deliver her final speech on why we should push our comfort zones more often in an attempt to motivate us all to take action. Within this brilliant speech, she posed a question that stuck with me for a long motherfucking time: "Did you do anything worth remembering yesterday? If not, why?" Holy shit. That got me thinking deeply about how I choose to spend my time, and for what activities I dole it out. That speech became the impetus for a lot of content within this book, and more specifically, this chapter.

Thought experiment time! This time, close your eyes, think deeply, and dig around in your mind palace for the one person in your entire life's story who exemplifies the characteristic of generosity. This is the one person who gives so unbelievably freely and without regard for any-fucking-thing other than the happiness and wellbeing of others. She or he is probably the first person to show up on moving day with a pickup truck, donuts, coffee, and maybe even a little something extra to kick up that coffee a notch. This is the person who, without even a smidge of hesitation, offers to pick up a shift for you at work, cover a class for you, or take notes when you're absent. This person is so frequently and disgustingly generous that you often wonder why you can't be more like this person, while it is that very quality that makes you want to be around that person that much more often.

Do you have that person in mind? For me, that person was a dude named Fred I used to work with in my life before college, and Fred, if you're somehow reading this, then you need to contact me because I owe you at least a beer or five. Now that you're thinking of your personal version of Fred, ask yourself if that person is weak, easy to take advantage of, or naïve and foolish. Are those the words you'd use to describe your Fred? If you're anything like me, and I know there's exceptions to this, so there's no need to correct me in some lengthy, edgy blog post, then you probably view your Fred as strong, caring, loyal, devoted, and literally anything but weak.

Us bullshit artists, I mean social scientists, define generosity as the virtue of giving something that has value to others freely, willingly, and without reservation, expecting nothing in return. What this means for the rest of us is that generosity is not the sole prerogative of the gift being given; rather, it resides more so in the attitude toward giving. The orientation of the giver toward the act of giving is altruistic and free from conditions attached. Remember the old adage, "It's the thought that counts," which is inevitably said after getting the absolutely worst gift of the annual office white elephant gift exchange? Yeah, it's sort of like that.

The gift itself can take many forms and need not solely be limited to a physical object with intrinsic value. Some of the greatest gifts we could ever hope to receive involve nothing else other than time and attention, which is, of course, preceded by the necessity of putting our fucking phones down. Through time and attention, we can give aid, encouragement, emotional availability, and sometimes, little more than a shoulder upon which to lean. For an act of generosity to take place requires one person to be mindfully present enough to recognize an opportunity to give, and then, for that person to freely act upon that opportunity out of a genuine sense of care.

For example, perhaps you're on your way to the local mall for some tacos and a new hair metal band tee, and on your way from the car to the mall entrance, in the reflection in the glass door, you notice a person walking behind you with full arms, struggling to hold a bunch of boxes. From there, you have a choice: you can either pause your forward momentum toward your taco and shirt mission to assist a total stranger by recognizing the difficulty with which the person is carrying the items, or you can ignore it, pull out your phone, and check Snapchat as you enter the mall. One choice demonstrates the simplest of common human decencies and the other is a supreme dick move. Generosity requires at least a sliver of mindful presence to be able to recognize such opportunities to assist others, whether stranger or friend. What's further is that generosity also requires us to exercise many of the other characteristics found within the pages of this ever-growing book, such as summoning our courage to act without fear of judgment (Chapter 5).

### This is Your Brain on Kindness

Medical science is pretty fucking amazing. I mean, a hundred years ago, we knew little about how germs caused illnesses, used leeches and opium to cure everything, and nobody could have ever imagined peering inside the human mind and examining what sections of the brain light up when we're acting out of kindness and generosity, but here we are. Immediately before doing something out of generosity, two distinct sections of the human brain light up like a Griswold Christmas: the area of the brain that is home to decisions with respect to self-benefit, or the ventral striatum, and the area dedicated to thinking about others, or the tempoparietal junction.

Holy shit, I feel smart now for using such big, expensive words, and I hope you do, too. Look how generous I was just then – I gave you these great big words to impress your friends. In no way do I benefit from such a gift, and I'm not even done yet. A third area of the brain, the ventromedial prefrontal cortex, lights up at the moment of making the decision to help out the poor fucker with all the boxes trying to get into the mall behind us. Try saying that five times fast, unless you're an MD or a pre-med student. In that case, you probably already knew all that shit anyway.

What the hell is the point of all this biological rambling? Well, when we choose to act generously toward other humans, the exact same parts of the brain light up as those that glow brightly when we enjoy really great fucking food as well as really great sex. It's true; the same parts of the brain responsible for eating and ensuring the perpetuity of our DNA also govern kindness toward others, giving us every fucking reason in the world to realize that this is a biological imperative. With this knowledge, it's no longer a matter of deciding to be nice to others so Santa will perform a little B&E and leave behind some goodies from the Sharper Image catalog. It's abso-fucking-lutely necessary to the survival of our species.

As if that's not enough, there's more. Participants in these studies actually decreased the physical dimensions of their amygdala, which is the region of the brain responsible for two of life's arguably shittiest emotions: fear and anxiety. Think about this for a minute. When people choose willingly and deliberately to act with generosity toward others, not only will it activate the same part of our brains responsible for the feel-great portion of gettin' some good lovin', it also decreases our potential to experience fear and anxiety in the process. Please, remind me again of any fucking reason not to go running out right now to do something generous?

### Chapter Challenge: Five RAKs a Day Keep the fMRI Away

You know those random acts of kindness (RAKs) we're always hearing about, like someone paying for a stranger's coffee in line behind them at Starbucks or someone leaving behind emergency coinage taped to the washers at the laundromat? Good, because now, it's your turn. There's even an international day for random acts of kindness: February 17. However, we don't need to wait for a pretend holiday to go out and do something selfless for others. Instead, as soon as you've finished reading this chapter, pick a day and commit to completing this challenge ASAP.

Your goal is to perform a minimum of five random acts of kindness in one day, though I encourage you to aim higher and do even more. Look, any dumb fucker can do a RAK and feel all warm and fuzzy and shit, but when someone sets out to do five or more in only one day? That's bad-ass, and that is when you're guaranteed to see a really fucking big difference in the way you feel, immediately and without any doubt. To get you started, here's a list of suggestions:

- Redo the guerilla gratitude activity from Chapter 11.
- At the grocery store, collect and return carts from strangers for 30 minutes.
- Compliment random strangers and fucking mean it.
- Write up "You matter because…" cards and hand them out to the people in your life, or better yet, do it for strangers in the mall.
- Call up an old friend or family member you haven't spoken to in a while specifically to tell them what you love most about them.
- If your parents are still alive, and you haven't talked to them in a while, give them a call (and this includes mine as well).
- Volunteer for an hour at an animal shelter. Bring a bag of dog food or cat litter with you to donate when you go.
- Buy a meal, bottle of water, and/or coffee for a homeless person. Better yet, buy socks, deodorant, soap, underwear, or other toiletries.
- Still better, go buy a fuck-ton of feminine hygiene products and deliver them to your local women's shelter.
- When you give items to the homeless, sit down with them, ask for their names, shake their hands, and ask how they are doing. Then, listen like you fucking care.
- Invite someone over for a carefully-prepared meal without expectation of anything in return other than great company and conversation.
- Pick up some flowers and surprise someone, particularly if that person would never expect flowers from you. BTW, it doesn't have to be just for a woman. Dudes like flowers too, and they don't always have to mean you're romantically interested.
- Take a broom to your local cemetery and clean off gravestones. If winter, bring a shovel.
- Write a letter to a deployed or wounded service member through Operation Gratitude or Soldiers' Angels.

- Write and mail a letter to a loved one, letting that person know you care. It doesn't matter if that person lives four blocks away; receiving a personally addressed and handwritten letter in the mail is really fucking awesome.
- Sign up for the bone marrow registry.
- Donate blood. Seriously, it's really fucking needed, no matter what your blood type.
- Purchase new toys and stuffed animals and drop them off at your local hospital for the pediatric ward.
- Leave a kind note, a bottle of water, and a snack for your postal carrier.
- Tip extra. Then, tip more. Make someone's fucking day.
- Pick up the check for a random stranger.
- Make an obnoxiously large colorful cardboard sign with a message emblazoned across it like "You matter" and then stand on a busy street corner and wave at drivers.
- Bring donuts or other tasty snacks for everyone at work.
- Write a love note to your partner and hide it somewhere you know they'll find it.
- Pick up a handful of $5 gift cards to coffee or even grocery stores in your area, and give them to random strangers.
- Offer to run errands for someone.
- Rake someone's leaves, mow their lawn, or shovel their snow. Probably best to ask first, though.
- Clean up litter by the roadside, at the beach, or at your local park.
- Leave emergency quarters taped to the washers and dryers at the laundromat or on the food machine.
- Send positive, uplifting text messages to five different people.
- Let someone or even several others go in front of you in line.
- If you notice a retail or service worker doing a great job, go ask for the manager, and tell them about it. Be sure to get the employee's name before you do.
- Turn your phone off when spending time with a loved one, and kindly encourage them to do the same. Be sure to tell that loved one that the reason is because you want to spend quality time together without distractions.
- Email/text/write to/message a former teacher who made a big difference in your life.

This should be enough to really get you started. If you did this entire fucking list in even one week, think about how miraculous you would feel by the end, and think about the size of the goodness ripple you will have started in your community and social circle. Spend some time really reflecting on totality of the experience. Tap into your newfound savoring muscles and reminisce on the best ones, anticipate each one, and savor those moments as they unfold.

Then, I want you to take a moment or two to ponder how your week would have gone differently if you had merely stared into a tiny fucking screen all week. Which outcome do you prefer? What the holy hell is stopping you from doing this all the fucking time? The answers are up to you.

# 15

# PUTTING THIS SHIT TOGETHER, CASSEROLE-STYLE

Here we are, end of the fucking book, and I've droned on longer than Axl Rose at the end of the Guns N' Roses classic, *Patience*, so I won't mince words and bullshit you any longer than I have to. This last chapter isn't anything new, but rather, it presents a concise series of reminders of the most important bits from throughout this entire fucking book. Think of this as a quick reference for the attention-challenged and something you could revisit often without having to re-read the entire thing, although my hope is that, through these activities, you are developing a stronger resistance to distraction and ability to focus.

**It's more important than ever for us to be mindfully present.**

Mindfulness is a deliberate choice. It's rooted in intention and the ability to *choose* to resist distractions and remain centered in the present moment, while also making ourselves available to notice the moment as it unfolds and take it all in without judgment. To do this, we have to *learn* how to make this choice in the moment. We live in a world filled to the fucking brim with distraction, and none of that is changing anytime soon. If anything, it's getting a fuck-load worse with each passing day, so it is an imperative of our modern lives to develop the ability to put the fucking phone down and choose where we direct our attention. Our loved ones will thank us for it.

**Everybody wants to be heard; it's far rarer to simply listen.**

Want to be a special fucking snowflake and be loved by everyone? Okay, maybe snowflake is a shitty choice of words, given today's political landscape, so let's rephrase that. Want to stand out among everyone else in your sphere and generate some real respect and love? The key to doing that is to simply fucking listen. There are enough miserable, narcissistic assholes in this world, all scrambling to be heard above the fray, but how many of us are genuine, empathic, caring listeners? Look, not everyone is going to be interesting, but how would you know if you never listen long enough to find out? At least understand how to switch off everything else, put the fucking phone down, and give the priceless gift of full attention by listening deeply to someone you care about. Think about how you feel when someone listens fully to you. Got that image fresh in your mind? Good, now go do it for someone else.

**Boredom sucks, but it's necessary.**

I like boredom as much as the next ADHD kid sitting next to me on any given day. I get it. It sucks. Boredom is uncomfortable, it's tenuous, and above all, it places some of us in a place of emotional turmoil, particularly if you're susceptible to such emotions. But, it's a necessary and valuable part of life! We *need* boredom to tap into our higher orders of creative thinking and get those juices flowing freely, so we have to confront it from time to time. I get how tempting it can be in moments of silence, when we've run out of all the things to do, to reach into our pockets and retrieve the phone, but seriously, put that fucking thing down and simply sit with the tension of boredom, even if only for a little while, just to see what comes of it. You may not develop the Theory of Everything all at once, but you might surprise yourself.

**Stop avoiding criticism and use it to your advantage.**

When you started this book, I bet you never thought you'd end up thinking about what a kickass exercise the Blind Spot Activity (Chapter 4) was, but if you're anything like the hordes of students I've worked with before, then that may have been one of the most meaningful activities of the entire fucking book. I know it was absolutely transformational for me when it happened to me unwillingly for the first time, standing on the steps to my shitty trailer back in 2003. Confronting what others don't like about us isn't easy, and most of us might just as soon avoid it like Walmart on Black Friday, for fear of ending up in some hilarious Christmas shopping highlight reel on YouTube. Just like with boredom, criticism is a necessary part of life if we want to develop stronger relationships with others, and you know what? I'd be willing to bet money on the fact that at least half the readers doing this exercise come to find out that an inability to put their fucking phones down was part of the problem all along, so if you don't want to do it because I said so, then at least do it for your loved ones.

**Throw off the shackles of inhibition and say "Fuck it!"**

The spotlight effect is real, and it gets in the way quite often, preventing us from living the lives we've always dreamed of living. In fact, when I think back to my four years in high school, my biggest regrets were: A) quitting band because I was afraid of looking like a geek; B) not asking out the girl I had a crush on because I was afraid of rejection; C) not dancing because I was afraid I'd look like a total fucking tool; D) avoiding parties because I was afraid I wouldn't fit in; and E) oh hell, I could go on all day, but it all has the same root cause. Every last fucking regret is based in the spotlight effect, and that's only my high school examples. It's never too late to push back and shatter the boundaries of our comfort zones. Within the last several years, I've sang on top of a bar, done karaoke sober, danced with my kids in public, worn ridiculous clothes in public without two fucks left to give, and drove around to deliver a concert to anyone walking down the street because the music was too good not to share. Those are some of my favoritest memories, and they never would have happened if I didn't put my fucking phone down and challenge myself to do something brave.

**Admit when we're wrong, own our faults, & seek forgiveness**

Next to wearing pajamas in public or shaving my head, admitting fault and seeking forgiveness ranks up there with one of the hardest fucking things I've ever done, but at the same time, such situations have been the most powerful when it comes to strengthening relationships. Each and every time I seek forgiveness, it removes yet another brick from my lead-lined backpack of guilt and shame. We are the only ones who can lighten our load, so to speak, and part of reducing that emotional weight involves learning to put our fucking phones down and invest in relationships worth saving. Accountability is strength made plain to others.

**Vulnerability is NOT weakness.**

Way too often, particularly among us dudes, we view vulnerability as revealing our soft underbellies, and while dogs may still view this physical act as a sign of vulnerability, we humans have clearly evolved beyond that. When we show our vulnerable sides, we're demonstrating to others that we place at least a modicum of trust in those people, and that trust goes a long motherfucking way toward developing stronger, more mature bonds with others. Put the fucking phone down, spend some time in thought on an emotional autopsy to revive yourself, and then go meet some new people!

**Savoring creates memories worth remembering.**

Starting in Chapter 8, we learned all about anticipation, savoring, and reminiscing, as well as luxuriating, basking, thanksgiving, and marveling.

Learning to savor the moment requires the ability to facilitate mindful presence, so if you don't have that going for you, the act of savoring will be really fucking difficult. Once you have that down, then the act of being mindful during moments of enjoyment and pleasure affords us the potential to prolong the enjoyment of that moment, sort of like a little blue pill for life's pleasures beyond merely sex (and not reserved solely for men). Learning to attend to that moment and prolong the beauty of what makes it so fucking awesome is the essence of savoring, and when we combine anticipation and reminiscence with that, we realize that, when we put our fucking phones down, there's a lot of life to be lived.

**Gratitude changes the lenses with which we view the world.**

When we pursue gratitude and take a few minutes each day to jot down that for which we are grateful, we have the power to shift our perceptions so dramatically that we may not even recognize life after such a transformation. All of a sudden, we're collecting things to be grateful for, rather than dwelling on and ruminating about life's problems. Instead, we're coping with those problems, addressing those bitches head-fucking-on, and resolving issues so that we can focus more on what makes life worth living. Research shows that pursuing a daily gratitude practice like the one outlined in Chapter 10 increases our potential for overall happiness and relational satisfaction up to the six-month mark, so the first six weeks is only the beginning. Want to change your life? Put the fucking phone down and focus on what's so incredibly awesome about this life we're living.

**Expressing appreciation is really fucking fun.**

Remember guerrilla gratitude? Well, if you actually followed through with it and did it, then of course you recall it. Not only is it deliciously devious fun, but think about how sickeningly wholesome fun it is! Imagine, for a moment, walking back to your desk in the morning, groggy from lack of caffeine, only to find a sticky note on your desk thanking you for being such a positive role model, great listener, and leader for everyone in your work group. Seriously, it's only one tiny piece of paper with an adhesive stripe on the back and maybe 1-2 sentences on the front, but something like that would make your fucking day. Research also shows that, as we increase our happiness in this way, it unlocks portions of the brain responsible for creativity, generosity, productivity, and intellect. I'll bet you'll never look at a sticky note the same way again. It all starts with putting the fucking phone down, picking up a pack of sticky notes, and setting out to make an impact in your little corner of the world.

**Taking back control of our attention happens incrementally.**

In Chapter 12, I made the case for using technology more mindfully as a means of reclaiming control over that which technology is actively trying to steal. From weekly digital detoxes, to consciously and intentionally manicuring our social feeds, to picking a fight with our assumptions and routines, these activities all work together. What we read, see, and hear on a daily basis has the potential to nourish our minds and souls in much the same way kale, Brussels sprouts, and all that other organic, non-GMO, free-range hippie bullshit nourishes our bodies. Taking back control is no simple, overnight success, though; it takes time, work, commitment, and a near-constant state of mindful presence to check ourselves before we wreck ourselves, to borrow wisdom from Ice Cube. In the end, we'll find it is increasingly easier and more effortless to put our fucking phones down in favor of life in the flesh-and-blood world, where memorable experiences await us beyond the limitations of a screen.

**Share value and stop comparing.**

In Chapter 13, I introduced us to the concept of the share-erang and the idea that what we share eventually works its way back to us like karma. If we share shitty, demeaning bullshit, that's what we'll see, which then feeds back into our conceptualization of reality. However, if I promote and share only that which has value, then the shittier stuff gets less views, likes, shares, and clicks, and I end up doing my part to clean up the virtual shitballs of the human litterbox that is the online world. We also need to get a grip on the fact that what we see of others' lives is only a tiny sliver of that life. People don't typically share the shitty moments, the fights, the complications, and the tribulations; they share the highlight reel. What's worse is that insecure people tend to inflate their lives online to appear even greater, when in reality, they're living just as comparably shitty an existence as the rest of us. Perhaps *they* need to put their fucking phones down and stop fronting. They need this book. Go suggest it to them.

**An act of kindness *will* change the world.**

The last activity was really an example of saving the best for last. If we all picked one day — just one fucking day — to go out and perform five random acts of kindness, imagine what kind of world that would become in a very short time. I know that, for me, when I'm the recipient of just one single random act of kindness from a stranger, it transforms my very fucking existence. All of a sudden, I'm somebody. I was *noticed*, and I matter.

On the extreme end, doing acts like this could even potentially prevent someone from committing suicide, should your random act of kindness coincide with such a person's trajectory at the right moment. We never know who we're going to impact and how, but one thing is for certain: kindness is never wasted, and it is the only commodity that doubles the benefit when given. So, put the fucking phone down and go do something nice for someone. I guaran-fucking-tee you that there is not a single goddamn thing on that tiny screen that could replace the joy you will experience when doing so.

## The Last Word

Putting the fucking phone down isn't easy, especially when most of us have become victims to the conditioning process that led us to this point in human history, so I want to sincerely thank you for taking this journey and making it to the end. The activities, supporting research, and my personal stories in this book weren't collected from a bunch of bullshit academic journals where over-educated brainiacs gather to make themselves feel smarter than the rest of us.

Granted, some of the research probably did come from such sources, but they were gathered by yours truly in an attempt to teach my own fucking self how to put my fucking phone down. Each and every goddamn activity in this book has been tested and tried by not only myself but also thousands of unwittingly coerced excitedly willing college students over the last decade. With each iteration, I worked closely with these students to refine and revise the activities so I could learn more about interacting with the world to make it more meaningful and provide ever-increasing depth.

So, on behalf of myself, my loved ones, and all my faithful, trusting students, I express my gratitude for having placed your trust in me for so many pages, unless, of course, you're one of those weirdos who skips directly to the last page, in which case, go read the rest of the book, freak-show!

I also leave you with my hope that this book and all the information contained herein provides a life-altering change, not only for yourself, but also for whomever you choose to share it with.

It's been a helluva ride.

Thank you.

# ABOUT THE ASSHOLE WHO WROTE THIS BOOK

Dr. Josh Misner is an award-winning communication professor, author, mindfulness researcher, and avid profanity aficionado (obviously) who missed the bus to adulthood somewhere around his mid-20s, yet continues to resist the urge to grow up. Josh currently resides in the inland Pacific Northwest with his undeservedly tolerant spouse and their brood of children and fur-bearing mammals.

A professor of communication at North Idaho College, alumnus of Gonzaga University, and TEDx survivor, Josh's writing has been featured in a variety of publications, including the Huffington Post, Time, and The Good Men Project. While authoring several books on a variety of topics, from public speaking to parenting, Josh's passion still resides in employing artful profanity to teach mindful presence as a means of achieving balance and cultivating longer-lasting, more meaningful relationships.

For more information, please visit www.joshmisner.com.

Made in the USA
Las Vegas, NV
24 January 2022